The Bates Theory

A Guide to Overcoming Toxic Mothers and
Male Co-Dependency

By A.J. Williams

Nation of Flame Publishing ©2020

Dedicated to:

The broken little boys inside us all, the men carrying secret trauma — and the pain that can't be explained.

Table of Contents

FOREWORD

The year was 1999, and I was in my final year of High School, which wasn't a normal High School by the way. Professional Performing Arts School, or PPAS, was a school for those who were already professional actors, singers, dancers and musicians. Since I had began my career in acting fifteen years prior, this was where I belonged. Even though my high school days were different from most kids my age (by this time I had a reoccurring role on a major soap opera, had done some actual operas, tv shows, and even voiced a cartoon character) I still cared about things that most boys cared about; girls, video games, and of course - television. Ever since I was on a set I knew I wanted to write and direct, and being a child of the eighties, television has always played a major role in my life; I have fond memories of Nickelodeon's *You Can't Do That on Television* and *Double Dare*, before the invention of Cartoon Network watching *Looney Tunes* for a half hour on school nights, *Teenage Mutant Ninja Turtles* after school, times at my grandmother's house watching *Murder She Wrote, Kojak, Matlock, Knight Rider, A-Team, The Equalizer, Hart to Hart* and many others, Saturday mornings watching *Inspector Gadget, He-Man, Transformers, Thundercats* and *Mask*, and Sunday nights with the family watching *In Living Color* and *The Simpsons*, which remains my favorite show to this very day. But little did I know that one show in particular would change the way I thought about my own childhood, my patterns as an adult, and my relationship with my mother.

I've been a fan of HBO since its inception. With my mother being on Broadway, and me being very responsible, I was left home alone quite a bit, and thus got to see this burgeoning network come to life. From the rousing opening theme when a movie was shown, to the network series like *The Garry Shandling Show* and *Dream On* (whose main character was a lot like I am in my adulthood, relating everything in his life to tv shows and movies he had seen as a child) to Comic Relief with Billy Crystal and Whoopi Goldberg, and even the first episode of Real Sex. I was there for it all. So it comes as no surprise that when the trailer for an upcoming series was shown, I was all over it. Well, in my final year of high school, a trailer was shown for a upcoming show one night that would change television forever. It was fresh, it was funny, it was violent and dangerous. That show was *The Sopranos*. The main character, Tony Soprano, was a New Jersey Mob captain in his 40's, who passes out from a panic attack. After finding nothing physically wrong, he goes to see a psychiatrist, who comes to help him discover all of the underlying, unresolved issues in his childhood which are causing him to pass out, and are ultimately the driving force behind many of his decisions. With its sex, brutal violence, and coarse language, it was undoubtedly going to be the coolest show on television, as me and my friends talked about it excitedly the next day, anticipating its debut. It did not disappoint. The writing was top-notch, the characters were exciting and richly developed, the in-depth look at the intricacies of family relationships, and the music and clothes brought a newfound interest into New Jersey culture, which as a born and raised New Yorker, I knew very little about. The show became almost religious for me. On Sunday, at 9pm, my family knew to leave me alone - I would even get off the phone with my fiancée in the years to come when the time snuck upon me without my knowledge. But it would take me years to realize why the show had meant so much to me. Was it just because the show was that good that I could not miss it, or was there a deeper meaning? I would later discover, from conversations with my wife and myself, that it was the therapy sessions between Dr. Melfi, played by the captivating and talented actress Lorraine Bracco, and Tony Soprano, played by the one of a kind talent James Gandolfini (R.I.P.) that were the most important. Their dialoguing and insights opened up a new way of thinking for me. I don't even remember if had ever heard the word therapy used in my house, or in any conversation for that matter. For those that don't know, the idea of therapy wasn't an option for most in the Black community, as it would involve opening up family secrets and putting behaviors on the spot, which is a no-no for us. When the show opens, it isn't too long before we are exposed to Livia, Tony's manipulative and controlling mother, who is already laying major guilt trips on him for even suggesting that she live in an expensive retirement community, which she calls a nursing home. It's one of her rants that sends him into a panic attack, and it was the first time that I had started to make a clear connection between a mother's behavior and a son's emotional state. It would become the baseline for this discussion almost twenty years later.

The title of this book is *The Bates Theory*, in honor of another iconic on-screen relationship between mother and son, the character Norman Bates in the classic horror film, *Psycho*. For those that have been on another planet, the movie was done in 1960 by director Alfred Hitchcock, and was groundbreaking in its own right; the opening scene shows the aftermath of a sexual encounter between a young blonde woman and a man in a hotel room, and that woman is later stabbed in the shower by an anonymous killer. The shower scene, with its haunting violin score and choppy cuts, became etched into the minds of any student of cinema, but it's the movie's backstory that grabbed my attention. Norman Bates, a young man in his twenties, runs a motel off of the highway by himself, living in a house on the property with his aged mother. As the movie develops, we see the relationship with his mother is a bit strained; even though she's never seen on screen we overhear him arguing with his mother about the new guest. But by the end of the movie, we learn the horrifying truth that not only is his mother dead, but he's pretending to be her as he carries out the murders happening in the hotel dressed in her wig and dress, and even when he has conversations alone! What would encourage such a mental breakdown? Why would it be wrapped around dressing up like a dead woman, and even going so far as keeping her body hidden away? In the final scene, a psychiatrist gives us some insight as the officers and family members of the slain victims in charge struggle to understand what they have stumbled on. He goes on to explain that Norman has actually come to assume his mother's identity as half of his own personality, and that sometimes that personality took over and dominated completely. But what was the cause of this radical mental breakdown? The psychiatrist goes on to reveal that when Norman was young, his father died, leaving him with a mother who was "clinging, demanding woman." For a long period it was just the two of them and they lived, in his words, "as if there was no one else in the world." But when she got a new man, Norman felt as if he had been usurped, so to speak, and killed them both. But his mother had left her mark, so much so that he felt the need to keep her alive after she was gone. Whenever he felt a sexual attraction to a woman as a grown man, the mother half would take over, being extremely jealous over Norman, and kill that woman. Now this is an extreme end of a fictional character, but we know that in many cases of serial killers, there is an abnormal relationship with their mother in their background, usually marked by some kind of odd or strictly religious upbringing, physical abuse or even sexual. Maybe these themes were deemed too risqué for the 1960's, as we never delve deep into exactly what kind of mother she was and what she did to Norman, but the idea was that their relationship was improper was definitely hinted at, and even explored further in a later series about Norman's upbringing. The point I took away from it was that Norman never had a chance at having normal, healthy relationships as an adult because of the unhealthy foundation laid by his mother. He would feel guilt if he ever tried to break away from her unnatural grip, because she had trained him that way. Sadly, I have seen this scenario play out with family members and friends.

My reason for writing this is simple; our men are dealing with serious psychological scars. Because many of us don't even know what they are, we can never fight them, and they lead us to make terrible choices as adults. If we are to ever break these cycles, we must first get to the root cause - our first teacher, safe space, bringer of care and love. *Mother.* Now as I write this, I realize this may bring major backlash, as all first attempts at truth do. More than likely, this will be branded as another attempt to "pass the buck" on the responsibility of men or worse yet, an attack on women. This is far from that. But many of us have been raised and trained as men not to question our mothers, or any mothers, for that matter. After all, how could we denigrate someone who carried us for nine months, went through the pains of labor, made numerous sacrifices for our development and well being? No one is perfect, and no one's methods are above being questioned and examined. Make no mistake - there are many wonderful mothers out there whose love is pure and self sacrificing, who are kind, thoughtful and supportive, who produce emotionally balanced adults. No. I am talking to the unprepared. The violent. The careless. The criminal. The reckless. The emotionally abusive. The physically abusive. The sexually abusive. The mentally unbalanced. Those women that should never have had children at all. This is for you, and the sons whose emotional states as grown men are a testament to

A.J. Williams

your monumental failures. Time's up.

-A.J. Williams

Introduction: Is Your Mother Toxic?

This question alone probably strikes fear in the hearts of most men - just the idea of questioning the person you have looked up to your entire life can fill a man's head with all sorts of questions and possibilities. But yes, the idea is more than possible, and very plausible. Before we can answer that all important question though, it would make sense that we first define what a good mother looks like. Now, most of this book will be devoted to examining a mother's role in a son's childhood, giving you, the reader, an opportunity to look back at your own and see if there are any parallels. But this question, is your mother toxic, is actually meant for the present time. For you see, if you were unfortunate enough to have been raised by a toxic mother, she's probably still very much in your life - and as harmful as ever. It would be good for you to find out if she is inflicting harm on you as we speak, so that you can have a flashlight to find the wounds she has caused in the past while you were a defenseless child - and thus, better understand who you are.

First and foremost, a mother is loving. But how do we define what that is, and what it looks like in the context of raising a son? Well, I was raised with the Bible, and while I realize that not everyone believes in it, it gives a pretty good definition on what love is.

"Love is patient, love is kind. It does not brag, does not get puffed up, does not behave indecently, does not look for its own interests, does not become provoked. It does not keep account of the injury. It does not rejoice over unrighteousness, but rejoices with the truth. It bears all things, believes all things, hopes all things, endures all things. Love never fails."

-1 Corinthians 13: 4-8, New World Translation

Now, what is described here is of course a very high standard - one that is impossible for humans to reach at all times because we are imperfect. But it does give us a baseline for examining the behavior of a mother. The decision to be a mother, first of all, is for the most part just that - a decision. A single woman, whether she was planning a child or not, makes a calculated decision to go through with a pregnancy and become a mother. When she does this, hopefully she understands that her life is forever changed, and she is now responsible for the growth and development of a helpless and defenseless person who will totally look up to her. The point being, since it is her decision, she should never "keep account of the injury". Does your mother do this? Does she use guilt, reminding you of all her sacrifices in bringing you up and having you to make you feel as if you owe her, and therefore can't turn her down in any way? Is she impatient with you - especially when you're trying to help or give advice? Is she "kind"? Or is she abrasive, difficult, mean spirited, closed off? Are you allowed to have important relationships outside of the one you share, or does she turn "jealous"? Must it be about her all the time, leaving her feeling threatened if anything, or anyone, seems to come between her and her little boy? Is it about her all the time - her needs, her feelings, her thoughts, trials and tribulations, without any regard for yours? Does she "behave indecently", getting herself into situations and conducting herself in a manner that is embarrassing to you, but without any regard for those feelings or remorse? Is it all too easy for her to become angry with you - her special little boy? Is it impossible for her to hear the truth about herself, much less accept it? Is she a force for negativity in your life, telling you what could go wrong all the time, or making you feel less than, belittling you? If you've said yes to any of these, and your mother is a big part of your life at this moment in time, then there is a good chance you have a toxic mother, and that means this book is for you. I've come to understand the dynamics of this relationship quite well over the years, and it is my true desire to help my fellow man come to understand and examine the true nature of their relationships with their own mothers.

For many men, this may be sensitive or scary territory, but don't despair. Many men shy away from discovering embarrassing or unflattering truths about their mothers. Is that true in your case? If so, why do you think that is? Are you afraid that you'll look at mom differently if you knew more about her inner workings and motivations? Are you afraid that perhaps, some of her failings as a person will somehow become a reflection on you? Those things may turn out to be true. But the question to ask yourself is why you would want a relationship with someone whom you didn't fully understand. What is a relationship like that really worth? That structure may be okay for certain types of bonds. We don't have to know everything about the people we work with, or casual friends we go to school with. We can have a perfectly healthy exchange with those we know only up to a certain point, but that is because those relationships have limits. Those people don't have to be involved in your future goals, your romantic escapades, or your home life. But your mother is different. Why? Because she is there from the very beginning of your life and more than likely, she's involved in many aspects of your life, if not all. Most mothers, if you asked them any details about their sons - even down to how they thought or would respond to a certain matter, would have no problem giving you an answer, and I would wager the answer would be dead on. With someone sticking so close to you, someone who is already 'inside your head' as it were, don't you think it's vital to know their motivations? If not, you could be opening up yourself to grave danger. *Danger from my mother?* The very idea might make you laugh. What kind of danger could I be in, especially from my mother? The concept itself may seem far-fetched, but think about it. When anyone new comes into your life, there's a period of examination - a 'checking them out' probationary period, if you will. During that time, persons reveal their viewpoints, habits, and inner thoughts. As they do, you can ascertain if their values line up with yours. If they do, you can choose to let them go further, giving them more access to your life and yourself on deeper levels. If they don't, you have the option to limit their access, only allowing them to reach a certain level in your life, and no further. You may choose to cut them off completely if the two of you differ too greatly on certain issues or in too many areas. Why would you do this? The motivation is simple: to protect your mental, emotional, and maybe even physical health. We choose the people that we want in our life, if we are discerning and endeavor to protect our peace. But mom is the first one there. We can't choose her. We can't even limit the effect she has on our life until we become an adult. So if mom just happens to be damaged, selfish, self-centered, manipulative, violent, or otherwise imbalanced, those negative traits are in her repertoire as she's raising us, becoming a part of the fabric of who we are, and we have no say so in the matter! That doesn't mean that those traits will automatically become our own, but they will shape the way we view things and how we interpret our world. It may be very late in the game by the time we actually discover how much our upbringing has had an effect on our minds and emotions, therefore shaping the way we treat people, what frightens us and holds us back, how we view ourselves, and so on. By that time, we may have inflicted much damage on ourselves, or on to others. If we want to build a better community and make sure that the next generation doesn't repeat old patterns, we must catch these things as early as possible.

So to our original point, a better understanding of mom is a better understanding of you. If you can get into her head, then you may be able to discover where some of those negative traits are coming from, and correct them. Better still, you can make sure the relationship between you and mom is mutually beneficial, and most importantly, healthy. Wouldn't that seem worth any temporary discomfort that some discovery might bring you? I would think so. Keep that in mind as you read. I wrote this for you. I understand you. I *am* you. This journey that you are embarking on is as much about self-discovery as it is about mom and her behavior. Once you can confront your feelings about mom, you can be real with yourself about them, thereby eliminating the conflict between what you think you're supposed to feel - and what things actually are. Once you have done that, you'll be well on your way to being truly strong - guilt and internal conflict free.

Chapter One: You and Me Against The World

In this day and age, it's undeniable that social media has become an integral part of our lives, although everyone has a different viewpoint on exactly how healthy it is. Some praise it for its virtues, while others condemn it for its vices. No matter what side of the coin you are on, one thing is for certain - we have access to more information than ever before, and in the realm of understanding people this is truer than ever. When it comes to mothers, they are ever present on these different apps, beaming with pride over their sons and eager to show them off to the world, as they should be. But it's in the language that's used that we can sometimes find the keys to some deep locks. Many times under photos of well-dressed young boys, we will find hashtags like "my king" and "me and him forever' or "me and him vs. everybody". What do these hashtags really mean though, and why is it important for us to examine them? The interesting thing is before there was even a social media to put these things on, they were being whispered in our ears as young boys, and even if they weren't said, the meaning that they carried was implied.

Growing up, my mother would tell me stories about my early

beginnings, and believe me, it belongs in a book. My biological father, whose name was Bernard, actually conned his way into meeting my mother in the first place, for it was actually his brother who was interested, but my father stole her number and address and showed up first. He must have been pretty charming to get his way into my grandparents house with a steak he then promptly started cooking, but that's the story my mother told me. At any rate, it wasn't long before they started dating, then living together. From my understanding, he was handsome and brilliant, charming, a great cook. But after a while things started to deteriorate. He would disappear for long periods of time, steal her money, sleep with her girlfriends... charming guy, I know. Drugs definitely played a factor. Because of this, many times he would steal the money she intended to use for the rent, or worse yet, steal her bank information and clean out her bank account. There were a few times when my mother was evicted, even though she made a great living as a dancer and actress on Broadway. When she finally had me, of course my father wasn't there, but there was a period when we were wandering around. My mother has told me on plenty occasions that she had to steal from stores to feed us at times. The point being, under that intense kind of situation there would undoubtedly be a strong bond formed between the young mother and her baby boy. (My step father would come on the scene when I was about sixteen months, and I will delve more into the effects of that in Chapter Six.) But even after he became a part of her life, it was essentially still me and my mom, and I would travel with her to the different places her show would take her, spend time backstage with makeup artists, stagehands and other actors as she performed on stage, or watch the show from the wings. What an exciting way to be raised, right? I have many fond memories.

As I grew older, my mom would often remind me of how much she loved me, telling me that no one would love me like her, and often referring to that time period and the bond that was built as proof - although I'm not sure if it was consciously or not. In either case, the message was clear. My mother and stepfather were married when I was about six, I started calling him Dad somewhere around there (I can't remember exactly when). The reason I bring this up is because even though I was fortunate enough to grow up with a man in the home, my mom still felt the need to remind me of the special bond of ours at times. Of course, there were complications to bringing an outside man into our situation, which would sometimes make this necessary, especially for her. I will delve into these later also. The point I'm making is, if she felt this strongly about our bond, how much more so would a single mother feel about it? How often would she remind her son that no one else in the world would love him like her? That he could trust no one but her? And with what intensity would she do this? In the interest of healing men, this is definitely worth examining.

In today's world, the definition of family is wide and varied. But in the opinion of many, a child needs the support of two parents for many reasons, the most practical being that the mother has needs and limited energy. One of the most natural needs that a woman has is for companionship, intimacy, and love. What if the mother is not married, and is not dating? That mother not only has to provide for the physical, emotional and financial needs of her child, but has to do so while her needs are not being met, or are seriously depleted. What usually happens to the child in a case like this? With all of that sacrifice, is it possible that they could still suffer loss in some way? And perhaps the biggest question is, with all of that at stake, why in the world would a woman choose to have a child without the proper support? Obviously I can't speak for every woman, but we are going to try to answer some of these. To stay on topic, let's first answer the question of what happens to the child. In a situation like this, the child will effectively become her man. They will start to confide in him, telling him grown up information way earlier than he can understand it. A son is different from a daughter in that, even though he is not ready, a young boy will try to step into the role of a man where he is needed because it is instinct, but also because he wants to prove himself worthy of the man he is destined to become. I'm sure we have all heard the phrase "you're the man of the house now", particularly in situations where the father has left the home - voluntarily or not. In any case, the son will try his best to provide emotional support and even physical protection, even though he is hardly equipped to do either. Men, *think back*. How many situations do you remember in which your mother was telling you something that you didn't fully understand, or couldn't handle, but you didn't say anything? I'm willing to bet you were thinking, I have to man up. She needs me to be strong right now. And how many times, even when you were a small boy, did you feel like you were going to protect your mom, no matter what happened? When a son supports the mother in stepping into this role, he further supports her in the delusion that he is more than her son, even if neither one of them realizes it. When she needs some emotional support, he's there. If she's ever in danger, the son might jump into a fight to protect her; in the home he'll grab a knife or a bat against a possible threat. Among men, this is perceived as normal, even proper behavior - the precursors to being a man. But is it? Don't get me wrong, I'm not saying that a son shouldn't protect his mother. I'm not even saying that he shouldn't care about her feelings or what she's going through. But the level at which he takes on this responsibility and the frequency of such gives insight into the true nature of that relationship. When these feelings are in a normal relationship with an emotionally balanced mother, or in a home with a father, these natural protective and supportive feelings can be guided in a proper way - and kept in their proper place. But in the absence of a father or mentally stable mother, they can be more harmful than good. What other dangers are produced from this abnormal relationship? From the son's standpoint, the line between what he and his mother are can't help but become blurred. They become more friends than mother and son, which seems harmless until the mother has to discipline him or put him in check. Now, our son is confused, and rightly so. The lines have been blurred, and in the absence of clearly defined boundaries, there is likely to be confusion. This can create resentment, as the child struggles to understand why his friend, who can cry on his young shoulder and promote him to a position of great maturity in one moment, can quickly reduce him to an underling in the next. Remember, a male child will try his best to step up to any plate, so he believes that he is qualified for whatever role you put him in. This can become even more damaging if there are other siblings, particularly if he is the oldest. If he is called upon to take on more of a parental role, this also skews his perception of who he is and exactly what role he plays in the family. He won't see himself as a child very long rather, he will begin to see himself as an adult and therefore, capable of making adult decisions. Unfortunately, there is another even more serious area that he can be led into with this - molestation. Many men, especially in the Black community, have reported that they began having sex at a very young age. Of course, these predators that took advantage of them were usually distant family members, family friends and babysitters. But what about mothers who are disturbed as well? No doubt there are countless, untold cases of mothers who behave inappropriately with their sons, as a result of having developed improper feelings for them that they didn't even realize they were forming. I'm sure you have heard, as I have, some mothers say some things about their young sons that if a father said about his budding daughter would be looked at as extremely suspect. With that emotional component thrown in, it's a recipe for disaster. And would a son in this position feel he was being abused? Most likely not, being that the mother has always provided him with affection, love and attention. He would most likely assume that the abuse is just an extension of those, as well as other forms which we will get into later.

What is the most damaging thing that happens to our young man, and how does it affect him as he grows older? For starters, his relationship with his mother becomes complicated from the very start. His feelings about her will be confused, and they will continue to be so when he becomes a man - even if he doesn't realize it. If he ever does happen to disagree with her, or wake up to feelings of resentment and hatred, it will be near impossible for him to exercise these feelings or communicate them in a healthy way because that bond has created an unnatural loyalty, which will then create conflicting feelings in him. Without the benefit of great insight or therapy, he won't know how to reconcile these feelings, and they will rear their ugly heads in other unexpected ways, such as resentment, violence and abuse.

If you are a mother, and you are concerned about some of these behaviors in your own relationship with your son, here are some questions you can ask yourself:

Do I share intimate information with my son?
Do I vent emotionally to my son?
Do I ask him to perform duties that would normally be the duties of a boyfriend or husband?

Ladies, despite what your situation may be, it is not your son's job to replace a man in your life, in any way. HE IS A CHILD!!! I know you have probably heard this more than once, but it bears repeating. If a boy is rushed into manhood, emotionally or physically, he is deprived of the opportunity to grow and mature naturally, which would allow him to shed childish behavior and tendencies along the way. Instead, he retains those tendencies well into adulthood because his growth has been stunted, and then we wonder why certain immature behaviors remain. That childhood will never be repeated so please, allow him to enjoy it. Many women, especially in today's climate, can talk extensively and eloquently about the qualities that they would like to see in a prospective man, or what attributes men should have in general. But how much do those things factor into the blueprint while they are raising sons? Do they see a connection between their conditioning habits and behavior and the future behaviors and emotional states of their sons? Definitely something to think about.

Chapter Two: Just Like Your Daddy

As I explained earlier, I'm a huge fan of movies. One movie that I always revisit is Boyz N The Hood, written and directed by the late John Singleton, who based it on his actual experiences. If you don't know it, it chronicles a young man growing up in South Central Los Angeles in the late Eighties, who is moved to suburbia with his father after getting into one too many fights in school. Unfortunately, this doesn't keep him out of trouble, because even though his father is responsible and teaches him life lessons and discipline, his peers have very different lives. In the beginning of the movie, when our main character, Tre, is about eleven, we meet his friends from across the street, Doughboy and his brother, Ricky. As he approaches the house, we hear their mother going off on a berating rant to Doughboy, "You just like yo Daddy. You don't do shit, and you never gonna amount to shit." You can tell from the context that Doughboy didn't just make her mad at that particular moment; this is how she talks to him all the time. In any case, it would be pretty hard, and pretty inaccurate, to sum up any eleven year old's life so quickly. Of course, we see she greets his brother Ricky with a warm smile and loving energy, so we know this isn't a reflection of her parenting or her ability to love, but rather her feelings about him specifically. Sadly, this kind of exchange is not confined to the movies. I'm sure all of us have heard that phrase "You're just like your Daddy" in our lives - if not directed at us personally, at a child that we knew. Granted, this phrase doesn't always have a negative connotation. If your Dad was a good guy or had good qualities, it's used as a compliment. When my mother has used it in reference to me, it was usually highlighting my father's intelligence, his ability to speak or make friends, be the life of the party - we even seem to share the same walk, I'm told. She never used it to denigrate me. But I could only assume that if I was a reflection of his good qualities, that I must also share his bad ones. When choices I made started to match up with his as I got older, it led me to question how much of his DNA really had an influence on me, seeing as how he wasn't around in any form. However, most children are not so fortunate. In any case, when we start to dive into these concepts, it can really get deep. How strong are genetics really? A question for another book, but in the quest to understand ourselves as men, worth examining, I think.

I've had the opportunity to see a number of young people grow up, and sadly, some of them were raised very poorly. One particular family comes to mind - three children being raised by a single mother. The oldest, a boy, a girl in the middle, and another boy at the end. The youngest seemed to escape her wrath and was a bit on the pampered side, but the older boy seemed to catch hell at every turn - and the relationship with the daughter was extremely volatile. Profanity and berating remarks seemed to be the norm when addressing him, and hitting him seemed frequent as well, but mixed in with that was also a heavy dose of neglect. It wasn't until I got older that a family member explained the relationship between the mother and his father was very volatile. For many of us in the Black community, this is nothing to write home about; I got hit quite a bit, although my parents rarely cursed at me. But our inner compass tells us when hitting goes from old school discipline to brutality, and there is something behind it besides just correcting the child. Sadly, I have seen this up close. There were times, as a child and teen, I pulled some shenanigans, as children will do. However, when it came to lying and stealing, which I did my fair share of, I would notice my mother become extremely wild - what I would even describe as violent. Whereas my father would just beat me with a belt, (although he would make me wait on the bed for him with my pants down, in some cases for a half hour which even as a young child struck me as a little sick), my mother could hit me with a closed fist, a broom, or anything really - even throw things at me on some occasions. This was hard for me to reconcile, because despite pulling some very normal teenage behavior I was a top student for most of my school career, and was very well-mannered. I was raised religious, and towed the line when it came to that, did my chores and I was super professional in my career. I could get hit pretty good for such felonies as rolling my eyes, talking under my breath, or giving attitude. But in certain cases, I could also get beat up. I always used to wonder where this kind of ferocity could come from, but I didn't have the psychological tools or the worldly experience to put it together. Just like our aforementioned son, I was the first child of a young mother, borne at a time of great distress for her, and fathered by a man who she was deeply in love with but who had done her wrong and abandoned her. If he had left wounds and scars that she would never get closure for, would I not be a constant reminder of his misdeeds as I grew in front of her eyes, looking more and more like him everyday? As I said or did things, unbeknownst to me, that reminded her of him, would I not trigger her pain and anchor her back to those very moments where he'd scarred her? What a heavy burden to place on a boy - one that would fail to exist if the pair was still together building a healthy relationship. Now of course, I realize that it is hardly a woman's fault if the man that has fathered her child doesn't want to stay, or is unworthy of staying. I doubt very seriously if my biological father would have been fit to raise me with his ways. But this is exactly why the decision to have a child is such a weighty one, and if you are in a sexual relationship with someone - even if it's someone you love, all precautions should be taken until you are both certain you are ready to have a child. The care of a son goes beyond buying him toys and sneakers. It is also about his emotional health, and I believe no woman could understand what it's like for a boy to grow up without knowing the person who gave you half of your DNA, personality, and qualities. For the men, I am hardly saying that you should stay with a woman if she makes it impossible to do so. But if you must leave, make sure you are an indispensable part of that child's life - not just for the physical support, but for the emotional as well. A man needs to know his origins, and with you present, he will know where he, and by extension, the rest of his family comes from. It wasn't until I got older that I realized how important this was for me, especially once I started having children of my own. Something as simple as questions from a doctor like, *What runs in your family?* can be a mystery. Or constructing a family tree. But most importantly, that relationship with the mother will stay in its proper place. You can show the right support for her, so that he won't have to. He will get to know who you are from his own experiences, not the stories of his mother that may be painted with the brush of a failed relationship, her own insecurities and God knows what else. Either way, he needs to know his origins. Of course, these suggestions only apply to present, responsible fathers. If he is dangerous or lacking maturity, of course it's your right as a mother to exercise caution and use your own judgment. But the fact remains that your son is made up of half his DNA - regardless of if he's involved or not. So it might be a good idea either way to let him know things about his father, and make sure they're the good points. Remember, the idea is not to make Dad look good where he's not, the idea is to validate the son. He identifies the traits that he has with himself before anyone else. When it becomes age appropriate, that might be the time to tell the negative traits about Dad, if you want to explain why things didn't work out - not as a bash-fest or venting for sport. Even though it may feel good for you, you have no way of knowing how your son might internalize those comments, seeing as how he is the reflection of the person you're deriding. Knowing about the other side of the family can be helpful too, even if they are not involved. Like the previous point that was made, if you want to tell them why they are not involved, you can save that for a time when you're sure your son is mature and won't blame himself in any way for their absence. But everything should be done to help your son have a healthy sense of his own identity. This is one of the foundations of becoming a healthy adult, and those shouldn't be made shaky because decisions of his parents. The main point to take away is, if you tell your son

The Bates Theory

he's just like his Daddy, make sure he knows why.

Chapter Three: Love and Violence

Men are probably more vocal in this present time period than we have ever been in history, and social media has a lot to do with this, in my opinion. It offers a place for people to talk about embarrassing or uncomfortable things from behind a computer screen, and even though it isn't the cure, I think it's a start. This kind of honesty is leading us to a healthier place. However, I have been in settings where men talk about their childhoods, even if it's only a brief comment, and it is shocking how many of us grew up with very similar childhoods - particularly when it comes to discipline. Some things I have heard were cause for laughter, like phrases that many of us heard growing up from our mother like "Do you have McDonald's money?" Or "I'll knock your ass into next week." Many comedians joke about such things, and even online I have read hundreds of comments in groups about mothers, where men from various backgrounds and ages would verify that they too had grown up hearing such phrases from their mothers. Some things I have heard though, were not so funny. Some things are revolting, shocking, and downright sad. Some of those stories came from a very close relative. This relative was the oldest of three children, whose parents divorced at a very early age. Sadly for him, it didn't matter whether he was at his mother's house or his father's because abuse lived in both places. From his father, he was beaten every day, no matter how he behaved - just in case he did something. Many different occasions were described to me, which I won't go into detail about, but that sound quite brutal. When it came to his mother, however, it would seem that psychological abuse was part of the parenting toolkit as well. Remarks were made about his appearance, and not kind ones - even comparing his looks to his younger brother's. In addition, it would seem that she was always sick. While I wasn't there, I am confident in saying that this was probably a manipulation - at least in part. What better way to keep a person whom you're mistreating by your side than be in dire need of him, keeping him loyal and subservient with a steady injection of guilt if he should ever even consider leaving your side. The reason I bring this up is because when the person that underwent this torture in his childhood was only twenty years old he met my mom and thus came into my life; surprise surprise - he had not attended therapy. It wouldn't be long before he was spending lots of time with me and my mother, and even watching me on his own. Needless to say, if he was interested in her romantically, he'd have to apply for the fatherhood position as well, regardless of whether he was qualified or not. Now my father, because of his strict and highly structured upbringing, brought with him many good qualities. He was hardworking, highly disciplined and organized, and religious - bringing God into our lives. He was also a highly skilled martial artist. As he would describe to me later in life, the neighborhood he grew up in was rife with gangs, and he was assaulted on a regular basis as he traveled to and from school. I don't know exactly when he began training, but he began teaching me things at about two years old; I won a competition not long after performing moves and using nunchuckas. As I grew older, he would study various styles for years to come: Wing Chun, Aikido, Karate, Tae Kwon Do and Muy Thai, and we would train in the house and in the park on Saturday mornings. In addition to watching him compete, there were quite a few instances where I got to see him use those qualities in real time. I have faint memories of a fight in a bathroom when I was about two or three years old, of him beating up at least three guys. It was a regular occurrence for him to pull people out of their cars in traffic when they cut him off, grabbing people up and threatening them - or worse. But there was one particular occasion that I'll never forget.

I'm not sure how old I was but me, him and my mom were in the car together, going into the city. As we parked, a vagrant started to approach the car. As we got out, he called us some kind of slur and spit on the ground in front of us. Before we could even have a reaction, a blur went by us as my father jumped in the air, and with a jumping flying kick sent the guy crashing through a store window. I had only seen that done in the movies; it was a magnificent display, and quite justified. But knowing Dad's temperament, this was just a day in the life.

In addition to martial arts being taught, it was also a major part of our entertainment, and my father brought lots of great movies into my childhood. While my mother was on Broadway in the early eighties, my father would walk me around 42nd street on his shoulders, stopping to watch the latest Chinese Karate flicks playing on small televisions in the cluttered kiosks around Hell's Kitchen. Many times we would stop into *Playland* arcade to play *Karate Champ* or *Street Fighter*. Visits to Chinese shops were also common, whose glass cases and walls were full of various knives, *shuriken* or "ninja stars", bo staffs, sais, nunchucks, and many other objects which excite a young boy's eyes. Many of these things we had at home. At home, Bruce Lee was a definite staple, as were Ninja movies with Sho Kosugi and Chuck Norris, Jackie Chan, and later on came Steven Seagal, Van Damme and other lesser knowns. I have very fond memories of all of these things, and many of them still have an influence over my life today; I thank my father for teaching me to defend myself at such an early age. But along with those great memories, are some pretty rough ones. My father could snap, and it wasn't just reserved for assailants on the street. I could get beat with a belt for practically anything, and a good number of lashes at that. I remember quite a few of them vividly. As I got older, things graduated to being punched up or thrown around. Being 6'2", muscular with a very serious disposition, this could be terrifying, and I spent much of my childhood being afraid of him. My mother however, was another story altogether.

As I describe things now, I always joke with my parents that my father's charges were federal, but my mother's were state. For those of you with no knowledge of the legal system, Federal sentencing guidelines are set numbers. For example, let's say for the purpose of example it was five years for gun possession, 10 years for robbery. There's no parole, no early release. You know what you're gonna get, and you do day for day. That was my father. I knew if I rolled my eyes, didn't answer fast enough, got smart, or got caught in school doing anything that would result in a call home or them having to come in, I was going to get a beating - with a belt. It was simple as that. But my mother was not that way. Different personality with different tactics. She was a state charge. When you get sentenced by the state, you could get a range of years, within which they have time to play with you. For example, you could get a 1-3 year sentence or a 4-10. Your eligibility for parole would come up, at which time you could be granted parole and released or catch a hit - another six to eighteen months. So you never knew exactly when you were going home, and my mother's discipline was much like that. She wasn't into psychological torture or staring me down to make me afraid. She might even let me slide with a huff or some kind of school trouble without much rancor. But when it was your day, the smallest offense could be the cause of an explosion. My mother would hit me with closed fists on a number of occasions, or throw stuff at me. She could get wild. The confusing thing was she could be so loving. For anyone that knows her or has met her they could agree; my mother definitely is one of kind - the kind of woman who takes control of a room when she walks in. She's beautiful, personable, always immaculately dressed (classy mixed with sexy), and always kind. So it would be hard for anyone that doesn't know her well, or didn't know her as a kid, to think that she could be capable of great violence. But that would be a mistake. When I was young, I witnessed her beat up people in the street just like my father. A woman who pushed me as we were traveling on the train. Another who got smart with her. I remember her beating some woman with her umbrella on the train tracks. Maybe New York's subway system just brings out the worst in people, but it wasn't limited to that locale. She has beat up friends and coworkers for various offenses, all of which I hope were justified. But because of her calm personality and easy disposition, I as a child was always caught off guard, and I'm sure her victims were, too.

Why did my mother have such a propensity for hitting, and why wasn't I an exception? Was she just prone to violence? Was it a childhood thing? When it came to me, was there a specific reason that she'd become unhinged? All of these are interesting questions to be sure, but the more important and pressing question is why is this so common - especially for Black sons? I'd be remiss if I didn't examine the fact that to Black men reading this, none of what I've described raises an eyebrow, whereas others outside of our race may be horrified. But that is not to say that sons of other races don't experience the same thing; I know for a fact they do. But why is violence so common by the person that is supposed to love us the most? When does it go beyond correction and discipline to something more destructive and harmful? Is this something that was even considered by the mothers of the past, or the mothers of today? I do know that I've seen many of my friends and family members grow up being hit with closed fists and objects, berated, left alone, brought to dangerous places, left with dangerous or child indifferent people, and neglected. I have heard many stories of them being whipped with extension cords, sometimes being stripped naked or being made to get wet first.

Switches, brooms, shoes, hangers or whatever object is near are very commonplace when men describe their upbringings. Now don't get me wrong. I have children myself, and children do need to be disciplined, but what we're describing here leans more towards cruelty than love, which discipline is supposed to be rooted in. A lot of these brutal tactics seem more like how an extremely cruel person would correct animals, or slaves - and with most of our family origins coming from down south, the connection seems easy enough to make. If masters taught their slaves discipline through beatings, torture and public humiliation, it would stand to reason that our ancestors adopted at least some of their ways and used them on their own children, which would be taught to our grandparents, which would in turn be learned by our parents. Of course, the main goal of such tactics was to instill fear and to maintain control, and it's no stretch to imagine that many parents used it for those same ends. In any event, it is not as effective as we have been led to believe it is, if raising good children is the goal here, and definitely not conducive to rearing emotionally healthy ones. This kind of violence is definitely the foundation for confusion in how the son will feel about his mother; the pain and humiliation of being physically hurt and emotionally degraded juxtaposed against feelings of love and closeness from the natural bond between mother and son, makes for one mixed up little boy. Of course, as we described in the previous chapters, a boy will try to rise to the occasion; he is dutiful, in most cases, so a mother won't see any resistance or resentment for quite some time - if ever. It may take many years into adulthood for a man to even admit to himself that he has any other feeling for his mother besides love and admiration, and even then, that's only the beginning. By that time, almost certainly destructive or self destructive behaviors have taken root in his personality, and are probably manifesting themselves in the outside world; anger issues, ulcers, panic attacks, violence towards others, criminal behavior, harming animals, drug abuse, alcoholism, and abusing women in its various forms: domestic violence, pimping, and even killing them. If you can believe it, there are even more ways a young boy can be affected by this kind of treatment; violence doesn't always have to be physical. What about the emotional, mental and psychological scars left by a mother leaves a young boy alone to fend for himself, either because she's a single mother working or because she is wrapped up in her own world? What is the impact of a mother who is emotionally immature, so when the pressures of rearing a child come, she resorts to beating or ignoring him because she lacks the skills to cope?

How can a son be expected to grow into a man that can communicate effectively, when he has been raised by a mother who curses at him and berates him? Lacks the patience to teach him? The costs of such inadequacy are innumerable, and the end results of these mothers are all around us.

The emotional demands of raising a child are extensive; no one is denying that. That is exactly why being prepared is so important. But it seems, especially within the last fifteen years, that having a child and raising it alone is not only commonplace - it is preferred. A mother pulling that load all by herself is bound to become frustrated and overwhelmed, and hurting the child will become the most likely response to those pressures if she doesn't have the tools or maturity to handle them. At best, she may just fob them off on a family member when it becomes too much, and who knows what kind of lifestyle or people they will be exposed to by extension? At worst, she may expose them to a dangerous lifestyle herself if she's irresponsible. If she pushes the panic button and brings a man who hasn't been vetted into the home, our young boy might be exposed to even more violence - or worse. But the dangers are not limited to single mothers. A married mother can be just as violent, or just as negligent. If we want to see more healthy young men who are strong, confident, and mature - it starts here. Our young boys need our protection, and they need to feel safe. A child is supposed to be born into a household where there is love and support already, established by two people on the same page, ready to cushion them as they grow up.

To my ladies, how you choose to live your life is without a doubt, your business. Choosing to have sex out of wedlock is your choice, living with a man unmarried is your choice, and if that man is not treating you right according to your standards, it is definitely your right to move on. But having unprotected sex while doing these things is a whole different ballgame. Having a child by someone who had no intention of being a father, and doesn't have the skills to be one is just reckless. And why would this even be done? I have no way of knowing, but after hearing the thoughts of countless women online I can venture a few guesses. A relationship is tough. Being with another grown person can be a vulnerable thing for some people - especially if they're underdeveloped emotionally. Many people don't want to be challenged in that way. Being in close quarters with somebody, they may want you to make changes, contesting the ways that have become the most comfortable for you - forcing you to grow before you're ready to. Even if they don't, perhaps their own advancement in different areas of their life shine a harsh light on your own lack thereof. I've heard many women say that they have no interest in dealing with a man who doesn't have his stuff together, who has too much baggage. It's too much work. But many of these same women have no problem raising a screaming, completely helpless needy baby - many times, more than one. They don't seem to be nervous about the prospect either, nor do they take any precautions against it. It can't be the work then, because it would seem to me raising a whole human being is a lot more draining than being in a relationship with another grown adult - especially if living with them is optional. So, what is it then? Well, let's examine first how a baby differs from a grown man. For one, a baby doesn't judge you. He looks up at you with love and admiration, showering you with adulation - no matter what. Regardless of what your failings are as a person, or a parent, you'll never hear about them or feel any judgment for them. You can also pat yourself on the back constantly for all the sacrifices you make as a mom, because you're doing it on your own. Everybody will make a big fuss over you as well, because a new baby is always cause for celebration, which is another big incentive for those feeling that they need a little boost, or are wrestling with self worth. Young girls in particular fall victim to this, especially if they lack love and attention at home, a new baby will give them plenty of both. Why else would a young girl with no money and no support be dying to have a baby, as so many do? She would hardly be equipped to deal with what's coming. They are the most likely to abuse their children, lacking the patience and understanding that come with years and experience, and none of us can deny the upswing in heinous torturing and murders of young ones that have been occurring of late by their mothers. All of this because of a burning desire to have a baby, regardless of the ramifications and damage that can come if the privilege is mismanaged. Secondly, a baby gives them something to love. If they are in a position where they can't find a suitable person, or many partners have left them, they have now found someone who will never leave them - someone to shower their love on. While the motives of these types of mothers might not be treacherous on the outset, the lack of balance that they have in their lives will and the desperation to have someone love them will ultimately prove to do more harm than good.

There is another way that this cycle of violence can shape a boy's life in a negative way. When a child feels powerless, he usually seeks to correct that imbalance himself, and he will do this by inflicting violence on someone else. Isn't it true that many times when we dig into the backgrounds of bullies, we find out that they were being bullied themselves? This might first start with a pet, as I mentioned before. Or it might be a younger sibling. If that is not available or maybe not enough, the child may move on to kids in school. Not just inflicting physical pain but dominating them, terrorizing them - causing them to feel the very emotions that they are so familiar with - humiliation and fear. As they grow older, those feelings will continue to grow -

and so will the scope of their victims. We have become all too familiar with gun violence in our neighborhoods and cities, and in the last ten years, our schools. These young boys that turn into violent young men have the roots of their rage planted firmly at home, if not directly from violence then from neglect. But what if their personality is not set up that way? What if they have a gentle spirit instead of an angry one? Those feelings of intense resentment over being repeatedly harmed will ultimately be turned inward, manifesting themselves into feelings of depression, worthlessness and maybe even the desire to end one's own life. How sad it is, the domino effect that acts of violence and neglect perpetrated on young men in the home can have, not just for the child themselves, but on our entire society. Ladies, if you are feeling the pressures of parenting begin to envelope you, and the father is not active in your child's life, I implore you to find someone to talk to - a family member, a friend or a spiritual advisor. Don't be embarrassed or ashamed about asking for help. Ask someone close to you (that you trust and know well of course), to give you a break. If none of those things are available or feasible, please call a hotline or get some professional help. Your child's mental health, well being, and even very life may be at stake.

I believe we as men are just all too familiar with violence. We grow up with it in our homes from strict, overzealous, and disturbed parents, we're raised with it in our cartoons, television programs, movies, video games and music, and we experience it in our neighborhoods and schools. But women have a complicated relationship with it. By and large, most women are not violent themselves, but many appreciate the security, safety, and company of a violent man - or at least one that is capable of being so. They cringe at the thought of a man abusing them, but will let their sons be beaten regularly. Many women are quite entertained by violent sporting events and other forms of entertainment. Upon examination, it makes for a pretty interesting psyche, doesn't it? I bring this up in this chapter because it begs the question, how are young boys turning into young men supposed to feel about violence? We are raised in an environment swimming with it, but society is surprised about the type of men that these sons grow up to be. And how are they supposed to feel about women after being raised in these environments? I've seen many women comment that this generation of men seems to hate women. Tupac himself said that "we'll have a race of babies who will hate the ladies and make the babies" on his song, *Dear Mama*. But the question is if that's true, then why? Granted, a percentage of these males can just be bad people, or those that don't fully understand women or themselves, and therefore treat them substandard. But why would they hate women? How could they come from a home, being raised by loving, caring, self-sacrificing mothers? I can guarantee you that most of them didn't come from those type of homes, that probably quite the opposite was true. I am willing to bet that most, if not all men who are misogynistic, violent, or indifferent to the feelings and value of women were forged in the fires of the mothers described in this chapter. They weren't born abusers or manipulators, they were made that way through years of systematic abuse. How else would they get this way? Now, there is definitely something to be said for the absence of a mature and emotionally developed father, which we've addressed in different parts of this book. Fathers are definitely charged with teaching a man how to properly treat a woman, so their absence absolutely has bearing in this issue. Examining that in depth is another volume, in another book. In the absence of good fathers, Mothers can be the gatekeepers of what comes into their sons' hearts by the type of environment they nurture. They can't do too much about the outside world, but they can minimize the chances of their sons becoming wife-beaters, child abusers, serial killers and violent criminals by making sure they are not bullied in their own homes. Our boys have enough waiting for them as men. Protect them and keep them safe.

A.J. Williams

Chapter Four: Perpetually Single

Initially, this wasn't supposed to be a book about women, but in examining the effects of the first female in a young man's life we can't help but focus on the habits of a young woman as she tries to raise that child. Now, we have touched on the fact that a mother who is married can be just as imbalanced, violent or neglectful as anyone, but those negative qualities are compounded immensely when the mother is without a partner. Let's examine a few different kinds of mothers in various circumstances, and how their approach toward singleness (single in this context meaning not being married or with a live-in supportive partner). Of course, there are many different variations and types, but for the purpose of this section we want to examine the ones that have the greatest impact on our young men coming up - and also the most common.

TYPE A: **Hard Working Mother**

Cynthia is in her mid-twenties, and her son Sean is about ten years old. She had her baby when she was still a teenager, and father left almost immediately, so she began raising her baby in her mother's home. But Cynthia is strong-willed so that didn't last too long, and finally she was able to get an apartment on her own. Being so young and not having the opportunity to finish school yet, she would only be able to find low paying jobs. Mom, family friends, and the ability to put her son in daycare definitely made the job easier, but she still has to live in a high crime neighborhood in a dangerous building. At first, her son is in no real danger; she keeps a close eye on him, has only trusted people around him (either family members or long time friends) and because he's small, he stays put at night. But as he grows older, the cuteness of him being a baby wears off, and she gets less and less help. Expenses grow, and she's determined to do better for herself, so she takes a second job in hopes of getting out of there. When he gets home from school now, Mommy's not there and he's all alone. She's a good mother, so she's given him strict instructions not to open the door or have anyone in her house, and he obeys - for now. When he's about twelve, however, his curiosity about what other boys are doing outside gets the best of him, and he makes his first venture out. He finds a few boys on the corners his age, and maybe a couple of older ones. They see our young man is a bit sheltered, and doesn't really know what's going on out there, but he's happy to be off the porch, and they can find a use for him. It's not long before they're giving him little errands to do, and now that he's getting older, he can see his mom struggling. He wants to do something to make both of their lives better, and since there's no other man to do it, it looks like he'll have to step up.

Let's look at this from another angle.

Dawn is in her forties, with a son Donald who is about fifteen. Dawn has a great career, and her and our young man live in a nice community in the suburbs. Dawn and her husband divorced some time ago, and even though he is involved, he is equally as busy. He figures that the expensive gifts and money should be enough to cover over the lack of quality time spent, and Dawn believes that because her son lives in a nice house and goes to a prestigious school, everything should be okay. But the suburbs, however exclusive, can be a dull place, and in a dull place teenagers seek to kill the boredom by any means. When Mom goes on her business trips, Donald throws wild parties in the house, or goes to friend's houses who do the same. Before long he is experimenting with drugs, and just as any curiosity, it begs for a greater thrill. Soon our Donald is addicted to hard drugs.

What kind of danger are our two boys in? The first boy, Sean, is in grave danger - danger from the violence in the streets, danger of being arrested by the police, and ultimately sent to jail. But there are other dangers as well. Our young man is in social danger. Learning his values about manhood and life from only slightly older criminals could fill his head with misinformation - or ways of thinking that can only serve him in that world, leaving him defenseless when he interacts with those from another world. He is in spiritual danger; the things he may be called to do on the street in order to keep safe, survive and make money will certainly stain his psyche, and when he finally wakes up from the intoxication of that lifestyle may look at his own reflection with disdain and sorrow, feeling that there is no redemption for him. There is emotional danger as well. In an effort to make himself as tough as possible, not to feel feelings of fear or sadness, or at the very least not let them show, Sean will learn to push them way down. He will also most likely lose the ability to form any close emotional ties, if he ever had it in the first place. When he grows older and tries to get into relationships, it will be very difficult for him to open up because he has been trained and taught that opening up will make you vulnerable - and for many men, that is a fate worse than death.

Our boy Donald, however, has some different problems. He's probably already deeply saddened by the breakup of his parents, and without a forum to discuss those feelings, is learning to cope with drugs and partying. He is also probably very lonely. A love affair with hard drugs can go nowhere but down.

The Bates Theory

TYPE B: **Living Her Best Life Mother**

Britney fell in love in high school, and remained in a faithful relationship for many years. They had a baby right away, a son named Eric. Even though she wasn't really ready to be a mother, she fell in love with her baby and threw herself into motherhood. However, her young boyfriend is not as enthusiastic about being a father, and the relationship begins to deteriorate. It's not long before he disappears, and Britney now begins to raise little Eric on her own. She is determined to prove she is a good mother, despite being abandoned, and is fully committed to buying her son the things she never had - designer shoes and clothes, and all the toys she can find. But she is also still young, and having missed out on her teen years raising a baby, she is eager to make up for lost time. She hits up clubs and bars, goes on late night dates, but she's not really ready for a new relationship yet. When she can't get a hold of Grandma, she holds the party at her house; she's not gonna let her kid stop her show. After all, she's a young girl, right? In the summertime when it's nice and hot, she's outside with her girlfriends, with Eric in tow. He's like one of the girls, entertaining them with fresh talk and curse words he's picked up from them, even though he's just a toddler. Eric gets a lot of face time with Grandma, who he begins to feel closer with as she pays him lots of attention, and caters to him but is most importantly, present. Grandma shows herself to be a grown up, carrying herself as a respectable lady and giving him discipline. Even though he's young, Eric can see the difference.

Karen has three children - two girls, and a son in the middle - Brian. He knows who his father is, but he hasn't lived with them since he was very little and is not very active in his life. In addition to being the only male squashed between his mother and sisters, the house is constantly filled with his mothers' friends and his aunts; in fact, the only male energy he gets to see are the random men that his mother brings around. Despite this, Karen and her son are very close. She's actually more like a friend or a sister to him; keeping him in designer clothes, helping him pick his girlfriends and even covers for him when thing get too complicated. There has never been a regular man in the picture, but that hasn't stopped her from dating - or bringing them home in front of her son. Brian is a teenager, and old enough to understand the motivations and hypocrisies of the women in his life.

What kind of problems might these boys have later in life?

Even though these mothers have different lifestyles, their sons will most likely share the same issues. For one, their mothers don't want to grow up, so even though they do adult things like pay bills and take care of children, they don't live the rest of their lives in a mature manner which includes separating from your children. Rather than be seen as a dusty old mom or a buzzkill, these kinds of moms blur the lines in a effort to be perceived as forever young and perpetually fun. While gratifying for the moment, what they don't realize is that their sons won't remain small forever, and may no longer look up to them when they grow older. Their morals may turn out to be different from their mothers, and as they come to understand the world around them more and more they'll be able to see cracks in the Madonna. This will create conflict within them as they try to balance the conflicting feelings of resentment and gratitude brewing within them. In addition, if a young boy sees men in and out of the home who are not his father, it may not have an immediate effect, but as he grows older and begins to form relationships with women it will. He'll begin to see his mother's behavior as disgraceful, but won't know how to process those feelings and as a result, will more than likely treat the women in his life with disrespect, disdain, and even violence. On the other hand, if he doesn't have those issues, he may be rendered incapable of making any decisions on his own - especially when it comes to his women, and this will be by the mother's design. We will examine this long road in detail in the chapter entitled "A Woman of Your Own".

Let's examine our third mother.

TYPE C: **Permanently Postpartum Mother**

Esther's situation mirrors one of our previous mother's, having started her sexual life as a teen, she got pregnant by accident, with no man to help her with the baby. Her mother has held her down though; seeing as she had her daughter in the same way, she could hardly preach to her. Being the oldest, she knows her way around diapers and bottles, and can take care of baby just fine. But without the emotional maturity and patience to go along with the domestic skills, things quickly go downhill. Her new son, who she has named Kayden, starts to put on pressure, crying nonstop, demanding to be fed all the time. This is normal behavior of course, but to a young teen it's an all out attack on their peace and sanity. At first, her way of responding is profanity - cursing and screaming at the baby. Her mother communicated with her in the same way, so this doesn't seem harsh or out of the ordinary. But as pressures build and the baby begins to get older, our young Esther graduates to pinching, sticking them with sharp objects, and even burning them. This may relieve some her frustration for a while. But as our young man gets older and bigger, he presents more of a challenge. After years with a steady diet of violence and berating, he's built up a bit of a tolerance to her, and may be defiant - either in words or in deeds. So she steps her game up, and begins slapping him in the face, beating him with objects, even closed fists. Does she feel remorse or even the slightest bit of concern about the way she parents her beloved son? Not in the least. This is how she has been shown you communicate with children. After all, she's raising a man.

Cherise however, is a bit different. She never wanted kids, and now at 21, she has one. After a couple failed relationships, she is feeling a bit abandoned. She's a beautiful woman, so she has no problem getting male companionship, but under that exterior lies some issues that no man gets to see - Daddy issues. Her father failed to express any personal interest in her, and she unknowingly seeks validation from the men in her life. Having sex, especially unprotected, makes her feel connected - so it's not long before she has a few more. Her firstborn, Aaron, feels the heavy responsibility of taking care of his mother emotional, as she is always sad or depressed. He also has the pleasant task of taking care of his siblings when she has taken a mental vacation; settling disputes, feeding them, helping them with their homework. Things get complicated between them, as they all have different fathers, so arguments are frequent in the house.

This is a big job for a 12 year old, but he never complains - even though he misses out on a lot of things that boys his age group enjoy. Despite his best efforts, it's not enough to help his Mom get over the depression, and she sinks farther and farther into a dark emotional hole. Will she drag Aaron and his siblings in with her?

These are cases where the boys are not only in emotional danger, but in physical danger as well. Kayden, the son of the first mother Esther, is in immediate danger; his mother is already assaulting him on a regular basis. In a case like this, there will definitely be a level of fear from infancy, but that will wear off as the child becomes older. As it does, he will also begin to realize that he is being harmed. He may not have the language yet to call it "abuse", but he knows something is wrong. Because he is internally programmed not to challenge his mother, those feelings of resentment that develop will be stored - and revisited at a later date. Trained in the art of bottling up anger and angry at being abused, it won't be long before Kayden starts to get into fights, taking out that frustration on others kids his age. As he becomes a man, that desire to quench his resentments will grow, possibly leading him to kill people. When he enters into romantic relationships, those issues will still be there, and as soon as the young woman he's with says something or does something that makes him anchor to his experiences with his mother, he will hit her - maybe even kill her. Young Brian however, may not have to wait that long. With a mother that never intended to have children, it's only a matter of time before her disappointment and feelings of lost youth will grow to consume them both. Many mothers feel the sting of postpartum depression, but it usually fades. With this kind of mother however, Aaron will never feel the natural warmth and connection that many mothers and sons naturally enjoy, and deserve. The news in our time is awash with stories of mothers driving their children into rivers, leaving them in burning hot cars, beating and stabbing them to death - or leaving them in the care of men who will the same. If a son was blessed enough to escape a mother like that alive, there will be serious psychological scars left behind.

Mothers, it is absolutely your choice to remain single if you have a child - and no one should make you feel bad about it. However, you should ask yourself if you have the emotional and mental reserves to handle the challenges of raising a young boy alone - successfully. The word successfully meaning that your son will remain emotionally, mentally and physically unharmed. Remember - no matter how strong your hold on him is, whether it be through fear or pity, guilt or friendship, he won't remain a boy forever. The return on your deposits of passive aggressive conditioning or brutal violence may have you withdrawing resentment and abandonment in your twilight years - or worse.

Chapter Five: The New Man

We've talked extensively about what parenting looks like under emotionally damaged and ill-prepared single mothers. But what if she decides she's ready to get back out there? What does that mean for her son? There are two types of suitors in this scenario - casual and serious - and they pose two different types of concerns.

Let's examine the casual relationship first.

A mother with a son makes the decision to go on a date and entertain a new man. No harm in that; Mom is grown and she has the right to have some fun. Everyone needs companionship, and single mothers are no exception. But what if those men start to come over the house? No matter what the age of the child, that imagery alone will have an effect on them. Maybe they will imagine that the man coming in will eventually be their Daddy; they have no idea what the nature of that relationship is. Depending on their age and maturity level, they may be quite conscious that they are missing a father, and may be longing to have one. If you are a mother reading this, and that is not your intention; you are just 'getting your life' as it were, keep it out of your son's line of sight. Unless it is getting serious, there is no reason for your date to see your home - or your children. Again, depending on your child's maturity level, he might know exactly what you're up to. Knowing that you're getting your groove back may very well change his opinion of you - especially when he starts dealing with women and being that guy himself. It's definitely something to keep in mind. But you might say, if you're a mother reading this book, what does that have to do with his life? This book is supposed to be about sons. Well, if it happens that he doesn't agree with your lifestyle, but he loves and respects you, he won't be able to tell you that. But that doesn't mean those feelings go away. They will reappear in his feelings and relationships with other women. He might grow up seeing women as just sexual objects. He might not see them as worthy of respect or value. He might not trust them. And he will never get help, because his life is being run by an inner narrative that you taught him, so his feeling will be normal to him - not something that needs to be changed or fixed. When he does attract good women in his life, he will most likely run them away for these very reasons, leaving those women to think he is immature, or afraid of commitment. So your actions have far-reaching consequences, beyond your immediate needs. So whatever you decide to do, as regards your dating life, please do it with discretion.

The Bates Theory

This brings us to suitor number two - the serious guy. For the purposes of this example, let's assume our mother did the all the right things before getting serious - and before bringing him around her children. She's vetted him, asking him all the penetrating questions about his childhood, his past, his goals and how he feels about children. She's watched him long enough in different situations to feel confident that he's not a weirdo, a sociopath, or otherwise untrustworthy. If she's considering her son's feelings, this conscientious mother will likely sit down with him and describe her relationship with said man, what her plan is for them - and ask how her son feels about it. No matter how thoughtful she is, or how well-planned, more than likely the son is not gonna like it - and there are going to be some issues. Right out of the gate, the man and the son are at odds without even meeting each other, because they will be competing for the mother's attention. I remember my father saying that I used to say I didn't like him - and we're talking about a two year old. A very *personable* two year old - whose personality was already such that he could enter into an adult career like acting. If a boy like that was saying that he didn't like Mommy's new friend, more than likely he sensed some things that maybe even Mommy could not. Not to mention that as time goes on, it's only natural that his presence will change the way Mommy deals with her son as the new man becomes a bigger and more intricate part of her life. He will start to impose his will and his viewpoint on how he is being raised, and what he would like to see done - and in an effort to please him, the way she relates to her son will change. Don't get me wrong. In some families, the right man coming along may provide structure, discipline and a proper male role model where there was none before. If he is mentally and emotionally healthy, this will all be done in a spirit of love and compassion, knowing that the child will only benefit from structure like that if he is assured he is loved first. But this will only be a blessing - and not a curse - if the mother does the aforementioned steps (waiting, vetting) and is strong enough and decisive enough to tell him when he should chime in - and when he should take a hike. My relationship with my mother was definitely less tense before my father came along, so even at a young age, I could feel the shift - and it only got worse. As time went on, I couldn't help but draw further and further away from her emotionally. I guess I felt subconsciously like I couldn't trust her - at least with my feelings. I became very private with those. I thought about all the times she watched me be beaten; all the times she witnessed me be humiliated and frightened and did nothing. At a young age, a boy doesn't have the language (or the balls) to question his mother about these types of things. Some of the ways boys *do* express themselves are fighting, stealing, becoming secretive, and many other departures from their normal behavior. We touched on the role of violence in *Chapter Four,* but in dealing with the new man in the home, I feel that it is worth revisiting. If there is violence as a result of the new man in the home (slapping, punching, beatings with a belt or other objects) it won't be long before the son you knew as a mother will start to disappear. As traumatic as those experience can be, he'll actually have an easier time dealing with him than you, because he'll know exactly how he feels about his Dad, but he won't with you. He'll just withdraw. But if you think this is one of those things you can just sit back and wait out, I'll have to burst your bubble; there are more troubles on the horizon. This man that has come into the woman's life - he may really love her, he may not. If he doesn't, and the relationship is just sexual or one of convenience, then that obviously doesn't bode well for the son. If he *does* actually love her, that is no guarantee that those feelings transfer to the son. The son was there before him, gets preference in the decision making (if the mother is at all a decent human being) and is a constant reminder of the previous guy - his biological father. So at best, even if he has fallen in love with him the kid is a problem - and one that will only grow as time goes on. Which brings us to sunny point number two. If our new man really cares about Mom and loves her, it's only a matter of time before he wants to have a child of his own, and of course Mom will be on board. When this happens, the family enters into a whole new level of complications. Right off the bat, the new baby is going to be more important - it's a baby. But more than that, it is new man's first child, at least with Mom, and therefore extremely special. Not only is it his own flesh and blood, unlike our boy, but it is also a symbol - a product of their connection. With all of that going on, our young man is bound to feel marginalized. I was a pretty damn special kid in my own right, and I still felt that way when my brother came along. So that just illustrates how powerful that kind of situation can be. Now if our new man is the conscientious type, he will have already anticipated these kinds of feelings, had discussions with our boy, and will be careful not to do or say anything that will make him feel looked over or discriminated against. Unfortunately, that is not most men. And Mom of course, caught up in the whirlwind of new love and a new baby, will be dismissive at best - especially if the child is in his teenage years. Now put yourself in this kid's shoes. He's already been abandoned by his biological father, for whatever reason, so there are underlying issues of abandonment and self-esteem. The new father, whom he's been forced to accept, is oppressing him and attacking him. His mother, who is his first line of defense, the safety net he has always known, is not preventing this from happening. Now a new baby is on the scene, so if he wasn't getting the right type of attention before, he's not gonna get it now. A big burden, wouldn't you say?

The issues that are birthed in this irresponsible situation unfortunately do not die as the child grows up; they only get more complicated. The relationship between the son and his stepfather will be strained - if there is one at all. He will definitely harbor resentment against the mother, and relationships with any subsequent siblings could be difficult. This is not etched in stone of course; my relationship with my brother is pretty good. But many brothers and sisters that grew up with different fathers find themselves in the midst of constant bickering and jockeying for position - even as they grow older. The arguments and disagreements they have usually don't stem from something based in reality, but rather have their foundations firmly laid in dynamics set up long ago by their mothers.

The burdens of our young man, unfortunately, don't stop there. In addition to being thrust into a new way of living in his own household, a new relationship with his mother whom he thought he knew well, bearing the physical and emotional weight of being constantly abused and/or humiliated, he now has to participate in the farce to the outside world that everything is well in the home. It becomes his burden - after all of the changes that have nothing to do with him and he gets very little out of, to put a good face on things. With all the pressure, all those feelings for years building without an outlet, it's hard to imagine that he knows who he is or what he feels by the time he's ready to leave home. One of the first problems he will have is a problem with authority. How does this translate? He's been taught by the oppressive and inconsiderate regime in his home that authority is unjust and cruel. He will learn that lesson elsewhere to be sure, but the important point to remember is where he learned it first. Therefore, he will always chafe when he feels himself being controlled in any way. This could lead to problems in school, and problems at jobs where you have to work under somebody. Now, a person reading this might say that is a crutch - an excuse for belligerent or otherwise disobedient behavior. But just think about it. Think about how powerful memories can be. Well, the subconscious is even stronger. Let's say a boss or supervisor talks to him in a threatening manner, or a girlfriend yells at him - speaking in a bossy tone. A tone that reminds him of one his father - or worse yet, his mother used. He will go back to where he was as a child - a time when he had no power and was very vulnerable. Because of that, he will begin to feel vulnerable again - now, in the present time. Not liking the way that feels, and not wanting to ever feel powerless again, he will immediately become defensive - maybe even lashing out at whoever is in front of him. Unless he gets help, this will happen over and over, probably resulting in many disrupted relationships and opportunities. But as we discussed before, how will he even know to get help? Before any of these eventualities happen, however, there will come a point where our young boy starts to become a young man, and the intimidation from Dad will begin to wear off. When that happens, it's a dangerous time for everyone involved. Frictions will begin to happen more and more often with the Dad, as the son comes in to his own and begins to discover a voice. But they might really come into full swing with the mother, depending on what type of personality she has. In my case, I very rarely got smart with my mother, because as I described earlier she didn't mind hitting. But if she's not that type of Mom, it's quite possible that the son will begin to challenge her more and more as all those feelings of resentment begin to bubble to the surface. Smart or biting comments can start to be the norm but it's not really about being a smart-ass or disrespectful as much as it is trying to have a conversation about what's been bothering him for the longest - he just doesn't have the words to convey the message properly yet.

There's no way to have zero challenges in the relationship between mother and son - no matter what side of the fence you're on. But you definitely should not make it worse. For the young boy, there's not much he can do unfortunately, except maybe run away - and I wouldn't recommend that. If you are the single mother reading this, it is your job to protect your son physically, mentally, emotionally and spiritually. Nothing and no one should get in the way of that. If you are doing that, then keep it up; I guarantee you will find rich rewards on the other side when your child is grown. But if you do a self examination and find that you have put things before your son, especially a new man, I would stop and redirect immediately. Depending on his age, you may have precious little time before your son loses all respect for you, and that would be a shame. For the fathers reading this that have sons, whether biological or blended, keep this in mind. Your son is a gift, a precious treasure that has been temporarily left in your stead. It is an opportunity to right the wrongs of your own childhood by being the man you never had, by teaching your son what you never learned. It is also an opportunity to step in and fulfill a role that is sorely needed, given up by someone who couldn't - or wouldn't - do the job. But if you're going to take that responsibility, you have to do it right. Merely providing in a financial way will not alleviate you from taking the lead emotionally and spiritually, which a young boy needs just as much. It is not a license to abuse and bully. If you do, the fear and resentment you create will ultimately override whatever lessons you may have to teach. Fear and hate can be a lethal combination, and you don't want to be breeding an enemy right underneath your own roof.

"One day the boy becomes a man - think he won't remember?"

-Frank Nitti, Road to Perdition

Chapter Six: Leaving the Nest

I t's natural for a young boy to begin thinking about leaving home at some point in his late teens to early twenties; a signal that he is ready to strike out on his own and get out into the world. I was ready to leave home at sixteen - well, if not financially or emotionally, at least mentally. That was when I felt that it was time for me to go, where I was starting to develop thoughts and feelings that were separate from what my parents wanted. I never went to college though; I left my career as an actor at eighteen to pursue a more spiritually focused life, so I didn't actually leave until I was twenty-one, when I got married. However, some men stay a lot longer, and whether they are working or not, have a woman or not, I believe the mother has a lot do with this. Now some men, are just not ready to go out on their own; many times, the issue is simply financial. But many men, even if they are good money-wise, feel they still have to watch over their mother - take care of her, if you will, even though she is a grown woman and has been for quite some time, not to mention just finished raising them. In this examination though, how the son feels is not as important as how the mother does, because let's face it - a grown man could hardly be on his mother's couch, in her basement, or in his old room unless she wanted it that way. And why might she want it that way? From the perspective of most, it may seem that she just wants to help her son out while he figures out what he wants to do, and that the son just wants to make sure his mom is okay - after all, he loves her, right? But let's be honest - there's nothing that a son would do in love and care for his mother that couldn't be done if he was outside the home; support, love, financial assistance, companionship, a listening ear, etc. A son that loves his mother is never more than a phone call away. No, there is something more dependent about them living together that late in life - something symbiotic. In many of these relationships, mother and son provide something for each other - security. A safe relationship with someone they've always known, as opposed to risking themselves in other adult relationships, as grown people do. With her son by her side, Mom will never have to grow as a woman, dealing with another mature man and living with him in a home. She won't have to take on the responsibilities that come with being with a man romantically and domestically, which might be scary for her. Instead, she can safely continue a relationship built on a foundation that was already set up years ago - and one where she has all the power. A side effect of this kind of situation is that it will stunt the growth of the son too; with his mom catering to him, he will never learn how to be in a proper adult relationship either. More than likely, whatever dynamics that were set up when he was being raised will remain, so he will probably not learn valuable things like compromise, leading spiritually, or just living with a woman that is not his mother - getting used to that energy and learning how to navigate with it. Now, many mothers do teach these things, and some mothers definitely drop jewels about how to treat a woman. But the kind of mother that would have her son sitting on her couch until his late twenties will probably only give pointers that are self-serving and allow him to manipulate instead of engaging and learning. This brings us to the next area - accountability. Letting a son live with her past the bloom of youth, so-to-speak, is not the only way that a mother can support a son to his detriment. He could be living outside the home and still be getting handicapped severely. She could be paying his rent in a separate place, paying for his car, letting him be on her insurance, buying his clothes, damn near raising his kids for him or just straight up giving him money on a regular basis. In a relationship like this, don't believe that she just wants to help him out. Everyone knows the "teach a man to fish" rule - that's how you truly help someone you love. No, in this kind of relationship the mother is exchanging money for something far more valuable - the son just doesn't know it. She is buying his loyalty. With all that payola, she is almost assured that she will have a die hard supporter and cheerleader herself - no matter what she does or how she chooses to live her life. Have you ever noticed how vehemently some stars will praise their mothers, attributing their success to their mother's dedication and hard work? But then when you actually do your research on their upbringings, you can find that these men had terrible lives as kids; exposure to drug use, prostitution, poverty, violence from inside and outside the home - much of it a direct result of choices their mothers made! How do we account for this lack of a connection made by otherwise intelligent, accomplished men? The only thing that makes sense, since a lot of the time we are dealing with intelligent, insightful men, is that there is a mental block there. A mental block cemented by systematic guilt and conditioning that will prevent a grown man from acknowledging the harmful behavior of his mother - even when the effects of it become painfully obvious in his own life.

The lack of accountability also goes both ways in this kind of relationship. Bad behavior by the son will most likely be covered up, excused, or even enabled by a mother like this. No matter what the son does, whether it is brought to her attention by teachers or family members, she always goes to bat for him, explaining away what he's done, or denying it ever happened. When the son in this kind of relationship grows older, he will inevitably relate how his mother had his back always - even when everyone else turned their backs on him. But did she really? It is in fact quite the opposite; if she shields him from accountability, she is preventing him from being able to grow to maturity. I'm sure we all know a few mothers whose son's can do no wrong. This can play out to be especially harmful when that son starts dating. In a normal, healthy relationship, mother would be doing her best to teach him how to treat a lady properly, but in an abnormal relationship she in effect becomes the son's wingman - helping him to maneuver to his own benefit. If there are children, she doesn't demand that he steps up and starts behaving like a man and father, instead she enables and facilitates his lack of growth by swooping in and taking the child off his hands, sometimes permanently. It is almost as if she assumes the role of nanny, allowing him to escape responsibility and continue his life as a permanent teenager. But let's give the young man the benefit of the doubt. Let's say a light comes on and he matures, finally realizing what he needs to do. He is ready to move out, and if there is a baby, he is ready to be a father on his own. How will the mother respond? Will she be ready to let go of her lifelong companion so easily, without a fight? If she does, how will she maintain control? Before we break that down, let me say this; any woman that becomes involved with a man whose mother is like this has her work cut out for her. We will deal with that in the next chapter, *A Woman of Your Own*. But back to Mom. She will try a number of things to make sure that, if her little boy does get away, he won't get far. One tactic is to make sure you're always needed. Now there's nothing wrong with a mother wanting her son's help every once in a while, but if you're a son who has left recently, chances are there's been an upswing in errands you need to participate in; drives to the doctor, putting up things like windows, shelves and lights, etc. There's nothing wrong with doing these things, but if it's to an excess, and seems to be increasing there may be a problem. What are the odds you're gonna turn her down after all she's done for you, right? All due respect, this would actually be a good time for a significant other to step in, now that you're gone. But I digress.

One tactic Mom might use is to suddenly become ill; nothing serious, just enough to keep you concerned. Every time you pick up the phone, she's "under the weather". But really she's malingering - exaggerating conditions, if there are any, in hopes that you'll run over and keep her company, or maybe just to keep her in the front of your mind. Now of course nothing is wrong with a mother wanting to see her son, even on a regular basis, once he's left the home. The problem is the manipulation. Instead of just asking to see him for lunch or something simple like that, there are tactics used to keep him in guilt or worry mode - thus keeping her first place in his mind. If she achieves that, he'll never be able to enter into any relationship more important than theirs - and that's what's most important to a woman like her.

Another tactic Mom might use to keep you close is by inserting herself into many of your personal decisions, not as a helping hand, but bossily taking over. Now you might ask, how can a grown man be bossed around by his mother? Again, the play here is psychological. Upon presenting your thoughts, ideas or lifestyle choices to her they may be belittled, laughed off, compared to a sibling's, or otherwise dismissed. This is designed to get you to question yourself and chip away at your self-esteem, so that you no longer trust your own thoughts but instead rely on her to make decisions for you. You'd be surprised how many sons actually live this way in their adulthood, but best believe that it has a strong foundation in their upbringing. The way she responds to you and your inner most feelings, thoughts and ideas will tell you a lot about if she respects you as a person. If she doesn't respect those, how could she really respect you? And if she doesn't respect you, how much can she really care about your well-being? These are sobering questions every son should ask himself.

Growing into a man requires separation; there are definitely things you have to change - and even give up - if you want to complete the journey into manhood. But to an unbalanced or mentally unhealthy mother, this natural growth spells the end of an era - an era where she controlled you, manipulated you, and could rely on you to carry out her wishes without question. She does not want to see that end. Be on the lookout for the tactics I have mentioned, and maybe others that are unique to your specific family dynamic and upbringing that might be made to serve her. Be careful about asking your male peers as well. They're more than likely are caught in the same trap, and may guilt trip you for even asking the questions, or suggesting that you don't dance to your mother's beat at all times. Remember, if you begin to signal that some of these behaviors are unhealthy, it may cause them to examine their own choices, threaten what they perceive to be benefits - and they might not be ready for that. Unless you see signs of separation in their own lives, let this journey be private. Many men believe that if you question your mother in this way, you are unappreciative of all the things she's done for you. But that's not so. In any relationship in your life, you should be constantly evaluating to see if that relationship is living up to what it should be, or if adjustments need to be made. The more you do this, the healthier your relationship with mom will be. But definitely get out of that house as soon as you can. It lends perspective that you can't get while you're under her roof, benefitting from her care. Don't worry - you can still have a rich relationship with her. But once you are no longer doing for each other you can see where you really stand, and you might be surprised - or horrified. On the other hand, it can lead to a place that is not symbiotic; a relationship based on two individuals, not what you can do for each other or what past struggles has bound you together.

A relationship based on respect.

Chapter Seven: A Woman Of Your Own

There comes a time in a man's life where he gets serious about a particular woman and wants to continue on the road of life with her. Depending on the woman he chooses, it can be a path to light, or a trail to darkness. When a man has a normal relationship with his mother however, and his mother is properly balanced, this can be a joyous time. For the man, he has a new woman in his life, one that he can build with, share things with and maybe someday start a family with. For the mother, her little boy has grown up, and is ready to start the next phase in his life. It is no longer Mom's job to take care of him, but it is now in the hands of a hopefully capable and caring woman, so she gets to relax a little, and hopefully worry a bit less. If she's normal, she should be ready to pass the torch, so to speak. But in a relationship like the ones we've been examining throughout this book, this is cause for alarm. The new woman is a strange animal that has wandered onto her territory, and is sniffing around her cub. The reaction is primal, and the response could prove fatal. Mom has cemented her life ally with consistent doses of guilt, abuse, pampering, manipulation, and conditioning - in many cases, a steady mix of them all. She's spent a lifetime grooming her son to be her perpetual right hand, and she's not about to let some strange girl come in and undo all that good work.

There are a number of tactics that may be deployed, all designed for one purpose: to get rid of little miss future happiness. Let's examine some of the ways that your toxic mother might approach this situation, and once we go through them, we'll talk about solutions.

The Offensive Approach

This is for the brusque mother; the confrontational, the outspoken. If this was *Golden Girls*, she would be Dorothy. What's coming out of her mouth is raw and uncut, so if you're the sensitive type, you'd better stay inside. A lot of guys think this is an admirable quality in their mothers; something to be celebrated. You'll hear them say things like "my mom don't bite her tongue" or "she always says what's on her mind", It's a pretty cute gun, until it's aimed at someone you love. This type of mother will say things like, "I don't like her." "She's not the one for you." "You can do better." You will be able to tell from the tone and the energy whether it's coming from a sincere desire to see you happy, or if degradation is the name of the game. Unfortunately, your girl isn't safe either. She may say things directly to her that are hurtful, inconsiderate, or just flat out cruel. Better yet, she might just say them to you, and leave you to figure out what to do with them. She may even say she is not welcome in her home, refuse to do anything with her or if she does, make it so uncomfortable for her that she is unlikely to want to do anything again. This of course, would put any man in a tough spot; do you confront your mother and defend your girlfriend, or side with mom? Many times, this choice alone determines the outcome of the relationship.

The Passive Aggressive Approach

This is just as hazardous to your romantic relationship as the previous assault, but way more subtle, so you have to be on the lookout. Think Ray's mother from *Everybody Loves Raymond*. The idea is to either get your girl to leave on her own or for you to dismiss her, but produce the desired result without leaving their fingerprints on it. The most effective way to do this is to plant seeds of doubt - the words 'seeds' being apropos, seeing as how they grow by themselves with just a little work. It could be what she does for a living, her appearance, her past - anything to get your wheels turning about the woman you chose, and if she's good enough for you. She might even suggest other women that would be a better fit - not by saying it outright, of course, but merely by bringing them up, or maybe even introducing them to you and setting up scenarios for you to be together. That's not to say that you shouldn't be having conversations with yourself about who your girl is; you should. A wise mother though, especially one coming to you in love, will know how to handle that situation without ever making you feel like she's trying to push an agenda. She will know how important it is to let you arrive at your own conclusions, so that if relationship doesn't pan out, it would be your own doing - and not the fault of someone outside. But a toxic mother has to be aggressive. She's working from a place of fear - fear that she will be replaced by this new woman, so she has to act fast. Undermining is another tactic, but this is more effective when it's applied to the girl directly. She might criticize her meals "This is how he likes it" or "I've always done it like this". She might even paint you - her son - in a negative light in desperation; remember, the point is to get her to leave you. She could start picking at your girl's self esteem, letting her know in a subtle way that she might not be good enough for you. Even worse, she could compare her to a former girlfriend - one whom she might still have a relationship with (You know which one). Of course, we can't cover everything here; Mother can be quite innovative with her years of experience and unhealed mental illness. But it's enough to give you an idea of what page she's on, and kinds of things you can be on the lookout for.

A.J. Williams

<u>The Malingering Approach</u>

There is another way that Mother will attempt to derail your new relationship; this tactic was mentioned in a previous chapter, although not in reference to this. Even though the concept is very simple, it is probably the most insidious of them all. There are mothers who will pretend to be sick all the time, whether exaggerating existing conditions, or straight up inventing them. What could be more bulletproof than convincing your favorite son that you're bedridden and in need of his help? What son would deny you? Now, to reiterate, I am not suggesting that every mother is faking, nor that you shouldn't respond to your mother if she needs you. No, this section is dedicated to those mothers that abuse that natural instinct to manipulate and keep their sons with them as much as possible. She could have already been doing this for some time, but with the introduction of a serious girlfriend, your bedside manner is about to change at the very least - and she can't have that. Keeping you for long periods of time, interrupting important events, or even holding you hostage on the phone can all be signs of a mother trying anything to take time away from your girl. As a son, any thought that your mother might be sick is usually cause for alarm, but once you get the sense that she is manipulating, the thing to do is to set some limits. You can make sure she's okay, but then you have to go.

Many men might fall out of their chairs at the idea of this; putting your girl before your mom? Well actually, it's not. This setting of limits on time and energy is not for your girl, but for you. If you don't, the relationship with mom will never be healthy and therefore, can't be truly loving. This kind of situation is not ideal for dating, but if it can't be avoided, it doesn't have to spell the end for your relationship. It's not for the weak or easily deterred, but it is possible for you two to come out stronger on the other side. The question is, will Mom go away?

A Tale of Two Queens

Let's say you've survived the dating period, along with your mom's shenanigans - and your girl has survived with you. You've even made it through the engagement period and managed to marry your girl without mom having a heart attack - or them killing each other. She is now your wife, and nothing can change that. You should be in the clear, right? Wrong. A toxic person doesn't like to lose, so the fact that her son has moved on to live with another woman means she has to fight even harder. The funny thing is, the angst will be all on your side, even though you're the one who wants to keep the peace. If your wife doesn't want to deal with her, she doesn't have to. If your mother doesn't care for your wife, she doesn't really have to see her. But you're stuck in the middle, and trust me - neither one of them are concerned about taking the pressure off of you. In this war, you're caught in the middle; you have to look out for yourself. Now, for those of us men that are old-school, we follow the admonition of the Bible; *"That is why a man will leave his father and his mother and he will stick to his wife, and they will become one flesh."* **– Genesis 2:24.** But with the proliferation of sex before marriage and women having babies without a man, it's no wonder that many men (and women) are confused about who comes first in a man's life, like I saw on one internet survey. The survey asked, quite simply, who comes first in a man's life - wife, daughter, mother, or sister? I was surprised at how many people said mother, although the overwhelming support was for the daughter. A man meets a woman, builds a life with her and because of that love and that union, the two produce a daughter. A daughter that is a helpless baby, but only temporarily. Soon, that baby will grow to a young lady, and that young lady to a woman, who will eventually move out and become someone else's. The mother, whom you've left to be on your own in the first place, should be busy with her own husband, or if she's single, a career and any number of hobbies and friends. But both of these women come before the woman you've chosen to be with - presumably forever? Seems crazy to me, but when you examine it closely, it really is no wonder why most people feel that way. In a toxic and abnormal relationship, the mother doesn't have a man, and has bonded herself to her son - and her to him. If a new man does come along, he will obviously be secondary, because the son was already there. The son gets the sense that he is the most important person (if he hasn't been told so literally), and with the messages that he will continue to get (both literal and implied) in his mind there will be nobody that can love him like mama.

Since so many men come up this way, and so many women raise them in this fashion, it's no wonder a large part of our society believes a wife is behind everyone else. They have no respect for her, or the position. But if you are a forward thinking man, you realize that putting your wife first is the `best investment you can make - providing she is a woman who appreciates and reciprocates that energy. Mom, regardless of the sacrifices she's made while raising you, can't fulfill the role that a wife can as you continue on your journey as a man, nor should she. Your daughter will provide an invaluable relationship, but the nature of that relationship is destined to be altered as well. The only one of these women who could stand by you for life would be your wife, so keep that in mind men, as you seek to prioritize. It doesn't mean you don't love mom, and it doesn't mean you don't value her. It simply means that you recognize, and seek to honor the natural order of things, not the twisted way things have become. Mom should have a husband so that she's not alone, that way she can be protected, and her needs can be met and fulfilled. If she's determined to stay alone, that is of course her decision, but there are consequences to that, and one of them is that someone may not always be there every time she needs them. If you endeavor to build a life with a woman, how could you possibly take care of her properly if you're always running to your mother's side - or if she never leaves yours? By asking yourself these sobering questions, you might bring some much needed balance in your life and I promise you, your wife will appreciate you for it.

Chapter Eight: Bastions of Bitterness

A lot of men are considered angry, and if most of us were forced to examine ourselves, it would be hard for us to disagree. Many of us are carrying around loads of residual anger. For Black men, we have the added stigma of being portrayed that way always in the media, and that's another cross to bear. For all men, anger is something we know well. But even as little boys we can manifest this self-destructive trait. If this wasn't us, I'm sure we can think of a few boys that have this disposition without even having five years on the earth. Sometimes, unfortunately, it's a birthright. Anger and tempers do seem to run in certain families, and many times parents will pass that on to their children. But anger, although a natural emotion, does more damage than it ever helps. More often than not, the most damage is done to ourselves. When we examine ourselves as adults, it may be fairly easy to connect the dots with our emotions, but remember we are getting to root causes in this book. So how do we prevent the next generation of men from letting anger dominate their lives?

It took me a long time to even realize I was angry. As a young child, I remember myself being quite happy in terms of my inner. A lot of what I was going through, and weight and significance of it all, hadn't really taken root yet. But I realize that my perception about anger also shaped how I handled it, even to this day. I've always felt that displaying anger in public, was crass - an act that belied a lack of control over one's self. Because of this belief, I trained myself to keep my feelings bottled up, and to nurse them. But not having a voice in my home contributed to that as well. It led to a pattern developing of me holding things - even to this day. What is dangerous about this practice is not only the internal hardships and risks to your health, but also the strain psychologically. You live inside your own head, constantly having the dialogues you wish you could be having with your aggressors. Even if you do confront people, which I learned to do, you still repeat the practice, because it's familiar. So this legacy of anger and harboring resentment is something that has far reaching consequences as well.

I've discussed my mom earlier, and anyone who has known her in their lifetime would probably never call her angry. But living with her and seeing her in those moments made me realize she must have been carrying something. Coming from a home with a alcoholic and abusive father, even though he never abused her, must have stored up some residual resentment for the way he treated my grandma in her early years. She was just too young to verbalize it, or maybe even know where the feelings were coming from. Even though my father remained calm in most instances, it wouldn't be a stretch to say he was pretty angry too. It's not that he couldn't be happy; he was known for outings and having a great time with family. But there was definitely an undercurrent. Like I mentioned earlier with regard to the presence of violence in the home, the presence of anger is just as pervasive. Many men have this in their origin story. That being considered, why is it that in society people are so confused about the negative behavior of men? It's almost as if it's we purposely don't talk about it - like a secret the family knows but everyone is ashamed of. I believe the reason why is because we know the damage being done to our boys in their vulnerable state as children, but in order to save them we would have to challenge the way things have always been done been by mothers, and there is still some apprehension about that. All of us know at least one little boy growing up to be an angry young man, and we know the household and mother he's coming from. Many times when we see this kind of young man and say amongst ourselves, "I feel sorry for that little boy", that means we already know there's serious turmoil and trouble going on inside their household - and inside them. We can already see the future coming. But do we step in? Do we really see the implications of raising a young man in a toxic, anger-filled environment - or one that is conducive to him being angry? We as a society have to start moving towards a more village-like mindset. How can we ignore day after day root causes that destroy children (our most sustainable future asset) and then be shocked and outraged at the horrific crimes committed by angry men, not making the connection at all? The environments sons are raised in count for a lot, too. Neighborhoods filled with violence and conflict are breeding grounds for rage and aggression, and most young men are raised in these. But even in relatively safe neighborhoods, anger is lurking behind well-tended bushes, waiting to possess a new victim. For a boy, it becomes more personal from pretty early on in their life. They learn a lesson about anger and aggression as soon as they have their first visit to daycare, or their first visit to the park. It is on a visit like this where they will invariably have an encounter with another toddler of choleric temper who will turn his ire toward him. Maybe he'll push him or take one of his toys by force. Maybe he'll bite him or hit him over the head. If he's fortunate enough to come from a peaceful home, he will learn for the first time that there are children who have a nasty disposition and will force that on you. If he comes from an emotionally unhealthy home, this will only reinforce what he's already learned all too early; the world is a dangerous place. Of course, if there is abuse in the home, or anger is being communicated as the regular language, that will only bolster feelings of anger and perhaps send the message that responding to problems with it is an acceptable way of life.

This is not to say that young girls don't experience these things, or that residual anger is an emotion that is exclusive to young boys only. But in the male world, violence is the currency - and aggression is the passport. If you have a calm or timid temperament as a child, more than likely you are going to draw the attention of bullies, who are determined to transfer their trauma to you. As a young boy, if you are absorbing that energy at school and at home, you are being oppressed. Oppression breeds resentment and resentment spawns anger. The average young boy is already walking around with all of this in his head and heart. It is very likely that if our young man was a peaceful soul, like I once was, that will change by the time he is a teenager. Many times when feelings of anger, rage, or resentment pop up a boy won't really know where they're coming from. But instead of talking about those feeling, which as young boys and men we've been discouraged from doing, our teenager will seek things that feed that anger rather than quell it. Violent video games, music that has anger and violence, and even violent contact sports might connect with the feelings already brewing inside him, but instead of exercising them or providing solutions, they reinforce them. I'm definitely not judging in this section because I've done all these things. In the interest of healing though, it is essential that's we begin to understand why we make certain moves and have certain patterns, if we ever hope to change them. So let's examine. A young boy who experiences violence and anger in the home, early on in life, while he's learning how to communicate, use language, and respond to the world around him. That young boy then goes to school, where he learns even more aggression; either by being bullied, or becoming a bully himself, exercising his own feelings in that way. In either case, he learns the lesson that anger and aggression are powerful tools, and a means to make people do what you want, as well as release feelings that are building up inside of you. With this steady diet of rage, what kind of adult can we expect him to be? In most families, parents are not chomping at the bit to take their kids to therapy to expel feelings of anger that they are largely responsible for. By the time he even realizes he's an angry person, you can bet that he's done a lot of damage already.

So how can we stop this cycle of anger and aggression from playing out in the next generation? One thing I believe is important is allowing your children to express their anger. Many of us come up in homes where expressing anger is viewed as disrespectful; depending on how it's done it certainly can be. But not allowing your children to express anger at all is denying them a basic human right - in effect, preventing them from being human. The problem with this is that while they might not express it for fear of you, anger is energy - and energy doesn't die, it just changes forms. The form that it takes could be harmful for your son, and for you. Creating a safe space where your children can express themselves is a major key to helping them become emotionally healthy, not teaching them to brood and hide their feelings. Be cognizant of the type of energy you have in your house. It would be good to ask yourself, what is the tone? Is it stressed? High-strung? Fear-based? Remember, your son will internalize the energy that you create in the place which is supposed to be their safe place. If they don't have a place to express themselves, they will definitely look for it outside the home. In today's world, that pretty much means online, and no parent wants that. In addition, they will more than likely replicate that tone in their own home involuntarily, or go so far in the opposite direction so as to avoid being you, that they harm themselves in other ways. The key here, is balance. Balance in tone, communication, and understanding. As a parent myself, I understand the challenges that we have in keeping it together. Managing stress and our careers. Managing the household. Maintaining our relationships. Disciplining the children. As a Mom though, you must remember the monumental role you play in your son's emotional development. He takes his cue from you in how to manage stress and deal with anger - especially if you're filling both parental roles. Even if Dad is really involved, odds are he spends more time with you, which means he watches you more. This doesn't let Dads off the hook, though. You are just as responsible for teaching your young king how to properly manage his anger. This vital piece of self control will go a long way in the success of his personal relationships, in business, physical health, and how he treats the women in his life. Let's do everything in our power to make sure our sons come out better, not bitter.

Chapter Nine: Slaying Your Dragon

Ilf this book has helped you to shed light on your relationship with your mother, and you have found it to be toxic, you have a decision to make. You can't save the childhood version of yourself from her, but what you can do is stop the adult version of the abuse, get her to confront and acknowledge her behavior, and demand that she change it. The first step, as regurgitated as it sounds, is being able to admit that something is wrong. You may not have the language, or a background in psychology, but that doesn't mean that you're incapable of identifying how you feel. You can start by asking yourself some very simple questions. After a conversation or a visit with mom, do you feel uplifted, or drained? Do you get the sense that she's building you up, or do you feel like she's using you? More than likely, you already know how you feel about mom - the tough part is just admitting it to yourself. It is possible though, to be so indoctrinated that you can't see what's happening to you. In a case like that, let's hope you have someone in your life who really cares about your well being, but is also brave enough to tell you about some things that may be out of place. If you have someone like that, listen. An outside eye can see things that you can't. After all, you stand to benefit way more from a closer examination of your relationship than anyone else could gain.

Now you've identified that something is wrong and you seek to change it, what is the next step? In my opinion, there is no cookie cutter way to address mom, because everyone's circumstance is different, and your issues with her are unique to your situation. However, I think the best thing to do if you have a mother like one that's been described in this book is to create some distance - some separation between you two. Let her know that even though you love her, you have your own life and it's important that she respect your space and time. If she can't do that, then maybe you should take a break from talking to each other. This kind of stance will let her know that you're willing to sacrifice even the relationship between you two for your self-respect. That will get her attention. The next thing to do is to let her know specifically about her behaviors. This is going to be hard. You're confronting an entity that is used to having all the power, whether overtly or covertly through manipulation, and they are not ready to hear what you have to say. A friend of mine told me his mother hung up on him when he tried to confront her with some of her behaviors. You can't make anyone be ready; you cannot do their work for them. But what you can do is set the standard for how you deserve to be treated, and how you want to be interacted with. You are the director of your movie. You decide who stars in it - and how much screen time they get. So remember that.

Now, if Mom is ready and willing to listen, the next thing to do is be completely honest with her. If you ever hope to have a healthy relationship, you have to get everything out in the open. You have to be completely candid with her or else, how would she ever make changes? When you've revealed all, be ready for any reaction. It's very possible that she will try to make you feel guilty about what you've said, because your words are piercing at that thick armor made strong by ego and conceit. Don't fall for it. She may respond with anger, taking you aback. Do not let her bully you. Remember, no one can dispute how they made *you* feel. All they can do is apologize. Any response beyond that is designed to make you second guess your own feelings, and ultimately let her off the hook. Another route she may go is being so hurt, so damaged by your words that she can't function. This is definitely going to tug at your heart strings, because that's what it's designed to do. Your natural instincts are those of a dutiful son, whose job is to protect mom at all costs - even emotionally. But think about it for a second. Think about all the difficult things that you've endured during your lifetime that you were able to survive and confront head on. Think about what you've lived through; the ups and downs, the different eras, the different disappointments. Think about all the uncomfortable choices you've had to make during those times - all the unpleasant conversations. Now think about your mother. She's older than you. She comes from even tougher times. Has probably endured things you don't even know about. You've seen her as a tower of strength your entire life. So how is it possible that this woman, forged in the fires of adversity and tested on the battlefield of life, can't handle a frank and open discussion about her behavior with someone she created? Doesn't make much sense, does it? The reality is that either she can and just doesn't want to, or she really can't handle it in which case, she needs to grow up. She is not taking the lead as she is supposed to in making sure that the relationship between you two is above board and solid, which as the parent, it's her job to do. One lesson that can be very hard to swallow is when you realize you are more mature than your parents in a certain area. If that is true in your case with regard to confronting things and making things right, you can make the choice to put it all out there, but realize that it is not your job to compensate for her. In the later part of her life, your mother should be mature enough to confront her harmful behavior and make changes - especially if that behavior is adversely affecting you. If she can't, you might have to bench her for a while. This may be painful but remember, just like some of the discipline she gave you when you were coming up, it's for her own good. Funny how life comes full circle like that. The point is not to be vindictive, though. It's really about teaching people how to treat you. In the same manner that your parents used to discipline you to teach you a lesson, it may become necessary to do the same in order to gain respect for yourself.

Everyone's outcome will be different. Some mothers and sons will come out of this difficult period with a stronger relationship, all the more closer for it. Some will never speak again. Still others will maintain a kind of shaky truce, where a remnant of the former relationship remains, but will never be restored. No matter what happens, remember that it is your mother's choice if she doesn't want to correct, or at the very least examine, her harmful behaviors. It is not your job to set the tone for your relationship, it is hers. If she is too immature for the job, or if she would rather choose the destruction of your relationship over fixing it and having it operate at its optimum, healthiest level, then so be it. Only you can watch out for your emotional well-being; if the woman who bore you won't do that, you can be sure nobody else will. The main thing here is not to feel guilty. Think of yourself as the reluctant gunslinger in the saloon, trying to give that loudmouth patron every opportunity to leave alive, but he insists on drawing his gun. What could you do? You can't let him kill you. In the old westerns, if a gunslinger was truly skilled, he would just "wing" his opponent - shooting him in the arm, hand or foot. You can do the same; figuratively, of course. You don't have to destroy mom, but set her straight and make your point. No matter what happens, at least you would have stood up for yourself and your principles, which is of course, the point of everything we do down here.

Chapter Ten: Are *YOU* a Toxic Mother?

Like I stated before, I wrote this book with my fellow men in mind. But that's not to say that I didn't anticipate women reading it, or how they would feel when they did. Let me reiterate; the purpose of this book is not to bash mothers. I salute and champion all the mothers who discipline without humiliation, sacrifice without guilt-tripping, and take care of their needs without putting their sons in danger. Men who are a product of those types of relationships almost always makes their mothers proud, and usually attribute much of their success to their moms. But the real question here is a sobering one. As you ingested the message of this book, hopefully you asked yourself one question continually - am I toxic? Well, nobody knows for sure but you and your son, but here are a few questions you can ask as well to help you see where you are. The first one is, how would you describe your relationship with your son? How do you see it? Seeing as how you are your son's primary source of love and protection from the very start of his life, there should be no reason why the relationship between you two should be anything but loving and close. If it isn't, that should be their first indication that something is wrong. The next question is, when you think of your dealings with your son, do you think in terms of what he can do for you? Is he your go-to person for all your problems and issues? Ask yourself how many times a week (or a day) you call your son - not to see how he's doing, but to vent. Then ask yourself if you're respecting him, his time and energy - or is your relationship more than a little one-sided? This is not to say that you shouldn't feel comfortable calling your son, or even talking to him about your feelings and worries. The concern here is frequency. If he is the only person in your life, or the first person you think of to unload your problems on, you might want to spend some time considering why that is. Relying on him so heavily may be taking advantage of him emotionally; if he's single, it may be hindering him from developing deeper relationships with others because he is consumed with you all the time. If he is in a committed relationship, or is married, then you are almost certainly affecting the relationship with his wife. As you well know, it doesn't bode very well for a man when his attention is on another woman too long - no matter who she is to him.

Another question to ask yourself is how you see your son. This could be the biggest key to unlocking why you perpetuate certain behaviors. When you look at him, do you still see your little boy

- the one you raised? When he was younger, you could control his life to a large degree - who he hung out with, where he went. You probably believed you controlled what he thought to certain degree, or that what he thought and felt was of little consequence when up against what your law was and what you had planned for him. But now he's all grown up. Is it possible that you are nostalgic for that time when he was young, so you subconsciously seek to make it live again, keeping him perpetually young as if in some kind of repeating Twilight Zone episode? I'm sorry to be the one to tell you this, but you won't be able to accomplish that. What you will accomplish is one of two things; a son that is never able to fully grow up and separate from you, and may therefore be hindered in the development of everything that is important to becoming a successful man: being independent, making decisions, finding and keeping a healthy productive relationship for himself, and so forth. The other option is that he does wake up one day, realizes how harmful you are in his life, and cuts you off completely. If either one of these scenarios is terrifying to you, I would suggest one thing - get help. If you have any type of trauma in your past; molestation, sexual abuse, physical abuse, psychological abuse or any other trauma, it seems the best thing to do is have those resolved before considering raising another human being. If you already have children, now you have a chance to undo any damage you may have done already by seeking therapy - and refrain from doing any more.

In all actuality, you really have to be honest with yourself.

What kind of relationship do you want with your son? Do you prefer it to be one where you have the upper hand emotionally? Do you like it one-sided? If you do, maybe you should examine why. Is it possible that you only feel strong when you are manipulating? Maybe you realize that if you didn't employ all the devices you have, your son might see you for who you really are... and leave you - for good. Coming to realizations like these may be painful, but there is no reward like doing work on yourself. You will come out on the other side stronger, with more self-esteem, and better equipped to have a truly loving relationship with your son, not one predicated on lies, manipulation, bullying, guilt trips, or any other trickery and device. You might even find that your son opens up to you more and you two become closer; he can bare his soul to you if he knows for sure you're not scheming in some way, or acting in a manner that will ultimately harm him. He can let his guard down, and be truly open with you. Isn't that what you want? On the selfish side, there is the added bonus of self-preservation; a son that loves his mother without being under duress is a lot less likely to want to get rid of her, and put her in a nursing home.

In today's time, all of us are fighting a number of wars on many fronts. Despite the turmoil we see and the divisions that have plagued us for so long, the only way to get to where we want to go is together. A place of peace, happiness and security. Where most people look for that first (at least down here on Earth) is family. But sadly, families by large are suffering, and they have been for a long, long time. There are many issues that they face, and most of us would ask 'What can I do about it?' Well, just like all other major issues that we all face, all you can do is your part. As a mother, you know the tone of your family - you know the pulse. If it's positive and loving, and everyone is close, in tune with each other, and operating from a place of peace and honesty, then you have done your job well, and I salute you. But if you are raising a son, and you have some of the behaviors in this book, it's time to stop. If your son is older and you already raised him with many of these behaviors, the good news is you can still do something about it. Apologize. Open a dialogue. Ask how he feels about you, and his childhood. Listen. Then make changes. Even though we can't change the past and the scars that we've put on people, we can alter our behavior and our understanding so that we don't continue to do harm. Don't think your too good to do it, don't let visions of your former hardships and sacrifices while raising your children convince you

you don't have to do it, don't be drowned out by oceans of self pity. Just do the work.

The benefits are waiting, because very few things are more loyal, more dependable, more rewarding than a loving son.

The Bates Theory

Credits

Psycho (1960)
Story by Robert Bloch
Screenplay by Joseph Stefano

The Golden Girls (1985)
Written by Susan Harris, NBC

Boyz N The Hood (1991)
Written by John Singleton, Columbia Pictures

Everybody Loves Raymond (1996)
Written by Phillip Rosenthal, CBS

The Sopranos (1999)
Written by David Chase, HBO

Road to Perdition (2002)
Written by Max Allen Collins, Adapted by David Self, The
Zanuck Company

About The Author

A.J., (born Amir Jamal Williams), was raised in Harlem, NY to a Broadway dancer, singer, and actress. Starting his own career in acting at the age of two, he began filming commercials, then landed a role in his first big show, A Different World, at the tender age of six. Since then, he has appeared in dozens of commercials, TV movies, theater, operas, a soap opera and even an animated series. After over sixteen years in the business, A.J. took on acting from another angle, directing his first play, The Diary of a Mother, in 2016, and it's revival in 2019. At the same time, he pursued a career in writing, releasing his first novel,

Flame of Retribution, in 2017 under his own imprint, Nation of Flame Publishing.

A talent for acting also comes with some other gifts: insight, the ability to listen, self-reflect, and to analyze. After examining his own relationship with his mother, the relationships of family members and friends, and countless conversations with single mothers and fatherless men, A.J. decided to put his powers and findings to good use. The Bates Theory was born - a book designed to help men pinpoint their feelings about the women in their lives, aid women in discovering the origins of questionable, frustrating, and dangerous male behavior, and help mothers understand the effects that their words, choices, and actions have on their sons - and the men they become.

www.ingramcontent.com/pod-product-compliance
Lightning Source LLC
Chambersburg PA
CBHW021406090426
42742CB00009B/1034